MOZZARELLA

Publisher *Beatrice Vincenzini*

Editorial Director *Alexandra Black*

Project Manager *David Shannon*

Art Director *David Mackintosh*

Design *Pentrix Design*

Project Coordinators *Emma Head, Rebecca Hayes*

Consultant *Francesco Moncada di Paternò*

Colour Reproduction *David Bruce Graphics*

Created by Co & Bear Productions (UK) Ltd.

Copyright © 1998 Co & Bear Productions Ltd.

Photographs copyright © 1998 Sian Irvine.

Printed and bound in Novara, Italy by Officine Grafiche de Agostini.

First edition

10 9 8 7 6 5 4 3 2 1

ISBN

INVENTIVE RECIPES
FROM LEADING CHEFS
WITH BUFFALO MOZZARELLA

MOZZARELLA

PHOTOGRAPHED BY
SIAN IRVINE

SCRIPTUM EDITIONS
LONDON · HONG KONG

Contents

Introduction 6

INSALATA / *salads* 14

PANE / *breads* 32

PASTA / *pasta* 54

LEGUMI / *vegetables* 70

RISO e RISOTTO / *rice and risotto* 106

PESCE e CROSTACEI / *fish and seafood* 124

CARNE / *meats* 136

Glossary 154
Contributors 156

Index 160

The Art of Making Buffalo Mozzarella

Above: Buffaloes arrived in the south of Italy from India in the sixteenth century, and locals quickly saw the advantages of making cheese with the rich, flavoursome milk.

In the terraced houses that line the winding streets of Naples, and in the farm kitchens of the rugged southern Italian countryside of Campania with its fertile volcanic soil, mozzarella has long been a staple part of the local diet. No one knows exactly how long the cheese has been made in the south of Italy, but as early as 60AD the Romans are recorded as making a similar food, curdling fresh milk with rennet extracted from the stomach of a sheep or goat.

Legend also has it that the monks of San Lorenzo di Capua gave bread and "mozza" cheese to the hungry who came knocking on the convent door in the third century. Eventually, the soft mozza cheese reputedly made by the monks became known as "mozzarella". The word derives from the Italian verb "mozzare", to cut off, the action of breaking the cheese curd into smaller, more manageable portions.

The transition of mozzarella made from sheep's milk to what is now considered the real thing – made from the creamy milk of buffaloes – came many centuries after the monks of San Lorenzo earned a reputation for their cheese.

Indian water buffaloes, which roam wild in southeastern Asia, were first introduced to Campania and other areas of southern Italy in the sixteenth century. They thrived in the mild, dry climate, producing a rich,

flavoursome milk from which the cheese-makers in the provincial capital, Naples, made buffalo mozzarella, or mozzarella di bufala as it is known locally.

Along with the region's passion for spaghetti, and its delicious plum tomatoes, considered the best in Italy, buffalo mozzarella became synonymous with Naples.

Over the centuries, the Neapolitans earned a reputation for their love of food and other sensuous pleasures. In the nineteenth century, when Naples became the fashionable heart of Italy, local dishes became popular all over the country. While those pursuing intellectual or artistic pursuits could revel in the antiquities of nearby Pompei or Pozzuoli, matters of gastronomy were best satisfied in Naples itself.

A stroll around the narrow laneways and markets in those days would reveal a banquet of tasty meals and snacks: spaghetti stalls serving up steaming plates of pasta topped with a sauce of succulent plum tomatoes; stands hawking savoury fritters and fresh seafood; the gelatiere scooping ice cream from his barrow; and, most famously of all, the baker plying slices of crisply baked dough topped with oil and herbs.

Pizza Napoli, as it has come to be called the world over, was baked in wood-fired ovens, initially only seasoned with a few drops of olive oil, a sprinkling of herbs, and perhaps salted anchovies. The dish had provided nourishment to generations of Neapolitans for at least two centuries before Italy's royal couple visited the regional capital in 1899, ordering pizza to show their solidarity with the people. According to local annals, the baker concerned wanted to add a little something extra in the couple's honour, so he garnished the pizza in the colours of Italy's flag: with slices of thick

Above: The best buffalo mozzarella is still made by hand, and is checked at each stage to ensure optimum taste.

white buffalo mozzarella, red tomatoes, and green basil leaves. He named it after the queen, Margherita, and the dish still bears her name.

Today, mozzarella is made in much the same way as it was when used on that first Pizza Margherita. Just as daylight is breaking over the gentle hills of Campania, the buffalo milk from the provincial farms is distributed among the small cheesemakers dotting Naples and the surrounding countryside, who make fresh mozzarella from it daily.

The milk arrives just after dawn and is poured into large aluminium tanks, allowing 4.5 litres of milk for every kilo of the finished cheese. The milk is heated to 35ºC for three or four hours and then a few drops of concentrated fluid are added to coagulate the milk, a process that takes about twenty minutes. The coagulant, called 'caglio', is in fact extracted from the intestinal fluid of

sheep when they are slaughtered, and is used to set the cheese, just as it was in ancient Roman days.

Once the curd has formed it needs to be broken up into smaller pieces, with excess liquid cheese being drained away to form the delicious buffalo ricotta. The firm cheese that remains is heated until it achieves just the right elasticity.

After three hours the cheesemaker selects a portion of the cheese and scoops it up with a wooden palette. If the cheese slides readily on the palette when hot water is poured over it, it is ready. If not, it goes back into the tank, to be tested again at five-minute intervals until it passes muster.

At this point the cheese is ready to be rolled into balls by hand, an art that is learnt over years of apprenticeship, and then soaked in brine for several hours before the whole process is complete.

Above: *Once the milk has coagulated, excess liquid is drained away to form buffalo ricotta.*

Above: *The experienced hands of the Neapolitan cheesemaker know exactly when the mozzarella has reached the perfect elasticity.*

Aficionados of buffalo mozzarella have their favourite makers, specifying a number of prerequisites that must be satisfied. The best cheesemakers usually run a small operation, with the freshness and quality of the cheese their main consideration. They should have been around for at least three generations, the craft having been passed from grandfather to father to son.

The maker should also be located fairly close to the farm providing the buffalo milk, no further than half an hour's drive, as the milk does not travel well over long distances. Most significantly, only natural ingredients must be used. Some larger manufacturers treat the fresh milk in order to extend the shelf life from a few days to a few weeks, but the resulting cheese is rubbery and tasteless.

Naturally made buffalo mozzarella only lasts about four or five days, and so the makers must ensure their product is speedily dispatched to the stores, restaurants and distributors they supply. The individual skills of the shop floor staff also come into play in creating the perfect cheese, but in the end the choice of a favourite maker boils down to the taste of the final product.

Freshly rolled mozzarella is at its peak just eight to ten hours after production when it is at its most elastic. It is certainly best eaten within a day or two, still dripping with the delicate, flavoursome buffalo milk. The mound of cheese should be glazed white with the sheen of the buffalo milk, and when sliced open should immediately reveal a trail of whey. It should still smell of the fragrant, lactic fermentation of the milk.

Cow's milk mozzarella is still produced in Italy and elsewhere, but cannot compare to the rich, moist buffalo version with its milky taste and soft, succulent texture. Devoured as is, with perhaps some slices of tomato, or a handful of olives, it provides one of the most delicious sensations of summer eating.

Francesco Moncada di Paternò

Above: *Fresh, hand-rolled buffalo mozzarella is best eaten within a day or two.*

Insalata

Dean Carr / THE AVENUE
Grilled Vegetable & Mozzarella Salad with Roast Garlic

Matthew Harris / BIBENDUM
Spiced Artichoke Salad

Lorenzo Berni / SAN LORENZO
Insalata del Principe di Napoli

John Torode / MEZZO
Roast Tomato Salad with Sorrel & Artichoke Hearts

Alberto Chiappa / MONTPELIANO
Insalata alla Sophia

Henrik Iversen / QUAGLINO'S
Warm Salad of Buffalo Mozzarella & Girolles with Cabernet Vinegar

Alberico Penati / HARRY'S BAR
Chilled Tomato & Bocconcini Salad

Nino Sassu / ASSAGGI
Aubergine Salad with Carta Musica

Grilled Vegetable & Mozzarella Salad with Roast Garlic

INGREDIENTS

serves 4

1 medium aubergine

1 medium red pepper

1 large courgette

1 sweet potato

4 baby globe artichokes

2 cloves garlic, chopped

12 cloves garlic, peeled

2 pinches thyme, picked

2 pinches rosemary, picked

1 lemon

10 tbsp olive oil

50 ml (2 floz) white wine

50 ml (2 floz) balsamic
   vinegar

2 x 50g (2oz) balls
   buffalo mozzarella

2 bunches rocket, washed

freshly ground pepper

METHOD

1 Fill a small pan with water and add the white wine, lemon juice, a splash of olive oil, one pinch of thyme, one pinch of rosemary and a clove of chopped garlic. Bring to the boil and leave to simmer.

2 Meanwhile snap off all the stalks of the artichokes and use a sharp knife to trim around the leaves, discarding all the outer ones. Place into the pan for about 6-8 minutes. Remove the pan from the heat but leave the artichokes sitting in the cooking liquor.

3 Wrap the whole cloves of garlic in tin foil and place in a preheated oven at 180°C (350°F) for 5-6 minutes until tender.

4 Grill the red pepper until charred on all sides, place in a bowl and cover with cling film. Allow to cool. When cold, peel, deseed and quarter. Set aside.

5 Slice the sweet potato, courgette and aubergine into 2cm ($^3/_4$ inch) pieces. Cut the artichokes in half and place under the grill. Once cooked, sprinkle with chopped garlic, a pinch of thyme, rosemary and olive oil to marinate the vegetables.

6 Slice each ball of mozzarella into 6 pieces.

7 To assemble the dish, arrange the grilled vegetables on a plate with the mozzarella and rocket leaves. Drizzle olive oil and balsamic vinegar over and around the dish and add the roasted garlic, finishing with a twist of freshly ground pepper over the mozzarella.

Spiced Artichoke Salad

(recipe on following page)

Spiced Artichoke Salad

INGREDIENTS

serves 6

4 globe artichokes

3 lemons

1 bay leaf

1 bunch thyme

2 onions, thinly sliced

2 tsp ground cumin

1 tsp ground allspice

1 tsp saffron strands

a handful of currants

6 tomatoes, peeled

9 cloves garlic

1 bunch coriander leaves

1 bunch flat-leaf parsley

3 x 100g (4oz) balls
  buffalo mozzarella

salt

2 tbsp olive oil

half cup white wine

6 slices ciabatta bread

METHOD

1 In advance trim the artichokes of all their leaves so you are left with just the heart and choke.

2 Place the hearts and chokes in a saucepan with 3 litres (5 pints) of water, into which 3 lemons have been squeezed. Also add half a cup of olive oil and white wine, a bay leaf, thyme, 6 garlic cloves and a pinch of salt. Cook for about 20 minutes. They are ready when a pointed knife goes in easily.

3 When the artichokes are ready, allow them to cool in the liquor and refrigerate until you are ready to make the salad. Reserve some of the liquor for later.

4 Before you start cooking the salad, remove the chokes from the cooked artichokes and dice the hearts. Deseed tomatoes, dice and reserve.

5 To make the salad take a large frying pan, add some olive oil and fry the onions on a medium heat until cooked just golden brown. Then add the cumin, allspice and 3 cloves of chopped garlic. While this is gently frying, heat up 25ml (1floz) of artichoke liquor and add the saffron to infuse. After a couple of minutes add the liquor to the frying onions.

6 Now add the diced artichoke and currants and stew for 3-5 minutes, adding more olive oil or artichoke cooking liquor if the ingredients start to stick.

7 Remove from heat, add chopped parsley, coriander and tomato, and leave to cool.

8 Meanwhile slice the mozzarella balls and grill 6 slices of ciabatta bread.

9 Serve a large spoonful of the artichoke salad on each plate, along with a couple of slices of buffalo mozzarella, a drizzle of olive oil and some grilled ciabatta bread.

INGREDIENTS

serves 4

400g (16oz) buffalo
    mozzarella treccine
    (or balls if treccine
    not available)

4 tbsp olive oil

2 avocados

4 ripe tomatoes

fresh basil

salt & ground pepper

Insalata del Principe di Napoli

METHOD

1 *Cut the avocados in half, remove the seeds, and slice.*

2 *Wash the tomatoes and slice them.*

3 *In the centre of each plate, place 1 of the small mozzarella treccine. On one side arrange the tomato slices, and on the other the*
avocado slices.

4 *Drizzle over the olive oil to taste, add salt & pepper, and garnish with some fresh basil leaves.*

Roast Tomato Salad with Sorrel & Artichoke Hearts

INGREDIENTS

Serves 4

4 oven roasted tomatoes

2 x 100g (4oz) balls
   buffalo mozzarella

1 bunch flat-leaf parsley,
   picked

2 shallots, shaved

1 bunch sorrel

2 marinated artichoke
   hearts

DRESSING

1 bunch sorrel, julienned

8 tbsp olive oil

salt & pepper

METHOD

1 *Overlap tomatoes and mozzarella in a tight circle around each plate.*

2 *Mix dressing ingredients and use a small amount to toss with the parsley, shallots and sorrel.*

3 *Place herbs on top of the tomatoes and mozzarella.*

4 *Drizzle dressing on top, season with pepper.*

Note: As a more refined alternative to the dressing, purée the sorrel, then add olive oil, to make sorrel oil. Season with salt and pepper.

INGREDIENTS

serves 4

100g (4oz) red oak leaves
   or radicchio

1 lollo rosso lettuce

1 frisee lettuce

4 plum tomatoes, sliced

100g (4oz) flaked tuna

4 eggs

2 x 100g (4oz) balls buffalo
   mozzarella, diced

$^1/_2$ red pepper

$^1/_2$ yellow pepper

salt & pepper

1 avocado

$^1/_2$ baguette (cut into
   bite-sized croutons)

4 tbsp olive oil

1 chilli

1 garlic clove

2 tbsp white wine vinegar

DRESSING

2 tbsp balsamic vinegar

4 tbsp extra virgin olive oil

1 tsp brown sugar

1 spring onion

pinch of finely chopped
   ginger

Insalata alla Sophia

METHOD

1 Carefully wash and dry all the salad leaves, place them in a large bowl, add the tuna, tomatoes and mozzarella.

2 Chop the peppers and avocado and add them to the salad. Season with salt and pepper and set aside.

3 Boil 1 litre (1³/₄ pints) of water, add 2 tbsp of white wine vinegar and a pinch of salt. Break the eggs 1 at a time into a ladle and lower into the water to poach. Set aside the poached eggs.

4 In a frying pan, heat the olive oil, add the chilli and garlic. Then add the croutons and fry until golden brown.

5 Mix the balsamic vinegar with the brown sugar, ginger and spring onions. Combine well, then add the olive oil and mix again.

6 Season the salad with the dressing and divide among 4 plates, along with a sprinkling of croutons. When ready to serve, place a poached egg on top of each portion.

Warm Salad of Buffalo Mozzarella & Girolles with Cabernet Vinegar

METHOD

1 *In a hot frying pan lightly colour the chopped shallots with a small amount of olive oil.*

2 *Add the girolles, season and sauté for 2-3 minutes, until just tender, add the shaved garlic and cook for a further 30 seconds.*

3 *Transfer the girolles into a bowl and add the mozzarella.*

4 *Return the pan to heat, pour in the cabernet vinegar and reduce by $^3/_4$, then pour over the mushrooms.*

5 *Add the chopped parsley, toss and divide the salad among 4 plates.*

INGREDIENTS

serves 4

2 x 100g (4oz) balls
buffalo mozzarella, cut in
half and sliced

250g (9oz) fresh girolle
mushrooms

2 cloves garlic, shaved

1 banana shallot

olive oil

salt & pepper

15g ($^1/_2$ oz) chopped
parsley

40mls (1$^1/_2$ floz) cabernet
vinegar

Chilled Tomato & Bocconcini Salad

INGREDIENTS

serves 4

300g (12oz) tomatoes,
   blended and strained

12g leaf gelatine

salt & pepper

200g (8oz) fresh tomatoes,
   cut into cubes

80g (3floz) extra virgin
   olive oil

16 mozzarella bocconcini

4 asparagus spears

4 baby fennel

1 bunch basil, finely
   chopped

chervil to garnish

METHOD

1 *Dissolve the leaf gelatine in water and reserve.*

2 *Mix the liquid from the strained tomatoes with a little salt and pepper and the dissolved gelatine, and refrigerate until set.*

3 *Boil the asparagus and the baby fennel in salted water. Drain and dress with half the oil and basil.*

4 *Remove the set tomato aspic from the refrigerator and chop roughly. Place a layer of the aspic in the bottom of 4 small dishes.*

5 *Trim the fennel and asparagus and stand several sections in the aspic, along with 4 bocconcini and the chopped tomatoes dressed with the remaining basil and oil. Garnish with chervil.*

Aubergine Salad & Carta Musica

METHOD

1 *Cut tomatoes into thick slices. Place on a tray on greaseproof paper. Sprinkle with salt and place in the bottom of oven at 150°C (300°F) and bake till dried.*
2 *Cut the aubergine into thin slices. Sprinkle with salt and set aside for 20 minutes. Dry the slices with a paper towel and brush lightly with olive oil. Place in hot oven for 3-5 minutes until soft. Sprinkle with basil if desired.*
3 *Sauté the aubergine in a nonstick pan, without any extra oil, on a high heat until golden brown on both sides. Remove to a plate and drizzle over a little olive oil and 1 tsp of balsamic vinegar. Shave the garlic clove with a potato peeler, and place shavings over the aubergine to infuse it. Add a little more basil if desired.*
4 *Cut the mozzarella into slices. Arrange the radicchio and rucola on the base of each plate. Place the bread on top of this, and then arrange slices of mozzarella, aubergine and tomato, alternating to create a fan. Sprinkle with basil and rucola, a little olive oil and balsamic vinegar.*

INGREDIENTS

serves 2

1 x 200g (8oz) ball
  buffalo mozzarella

2 large, ripe vine tomatoes

1 small aubergine

2 sheets Carta Musica
  flatbread (soften by
  sprinkling with water and
  shaking off excess)

1 radicchio

1 rucola

2 tbsp extra virgin
  olive oil

2 tsp balsamic vinegar

1 clove garlic

handful of chopped basil

Pane

Michael Moore / BLUEBIRD

Flatbread with Bocconcini, Spices & Anchovies

David Burke / LE PONT DE LA TOUR

Panfried Ciabatta Sandwich with Buffalo Mozzarella

Antonello Tagliabue / BICE

Focaccia Toscana with Mozzarella, Roasted Peppers & Basil Cream

John Torode / MEZZO

Brioche with Peppers, Aubergines & Mozzarella

Paul Wilson / GEORGE'S

Crescenta of Mozzarella & Roasted Peppers with Anchoiade

Sally Clarke / CLARKE'S

Baked Shallot & Oven Dried Tomato Focaccia with Bocconcini

Michael Moore / BLUEBIRD

Rotolo of Woodroasted Aubergine with Peppers & Brioche

Alastair Little / ALASTAIR LITTLE

Focaccia with Buffalo Mozzarella & Rosemary

Michael Moore / BLUEBIRD

Polenta, Mozzarella & Parma Ham Sandwich

INGREDIENTS

serves 4

500g (1lb) flour

1 tsp bicarbonate of soda

2 tsp dried yeast

300mls (12floz) warm
    water

1 egg

$^1/_2$ tsp sugar

50ml (2floz) olive oil

15g ($^1/_2$oz) fennel seeds

sea salt

black pepper

20 small black grapes

TOPPING

200g (8oz) buffalo
    mozzarella bocconcini

30g (1oz) anchovies

$^1/_2$ bunch flat-leaf parsley

20g ($^1/_2$oz) fine salted
    capers (washed)

Flatbread with Bocconcini, Spices & Anchovies

METHOD

1 *Mix the yeast, sugar and warm water together for 4 minutes.*

2 *Place the flour and bicarbonate of soda together in a separate bowl.*

3 *Beat the egg and add to the yeast, then combine with the flour using a mixer on a slow speed.*

4 *Add the olive oil and mix for a further 3 minutes until smooth.*

5 *Cover the bowl with a wet cloth and leave the dough to prove for 20 minutes.*

6 *Knead the dough briefly then separate into 100g (4oz) balls. Shape the balls as for a pizza base.*

7 *Brush with olive oil, sprinkle with fennel seeds, salt, pepper and grapes. Leave to rise for 10 minutes.*

8 *Bake in a hot oven for 8 minutes.*

9 *Meanwhile roughly chop together the anchovies, capers and parsley.*

10 *When the bread is cooked, slice the bocconcini onto it, sprinkle the parsley mixture over, drizzle with olive oil and serve.*

Note: This dish may be served warm or cold. To warm, place in the oven or under grill for 2 minutes before dressing.

Pan Fried Ciabatta Sandwich with Buffalo Mozzarella

METHOD

1 *Place each slice of Parma ham on a slice of ciabatta so that it overhangs the bread.*

2 *Cut the mozzarella into 12 even slices and place 3 pieces on top of each Parma ham slice.*

3 *Fold the overhanging Parma ham up and over the mozzarella to form an envelope and place the remaining slice of ciabatta on top, pressing down gently.*

4 *In a heavy-bottomed pan, heat a little olive oil. When the oil is hot, dip each sandwich in egg on both sides and place in the pan. Cook evenly on both sides until golden brown, with the mozzarella slightly melting.*

5 *Serve immediately with a simple dressed salad.*

INGREDIENTS

Serves 4

2 x 100g (4oz) balls buffalo mozzarella

4 thin slices Parma ham

1 loaf ciabatta bread, cut into 8 sandwich-sized slices

4 large whole eggs, beaten & seasoned

2 tbsp olive oil

Focaccia Toscana with Mozzarella, Roasted Peppers & Basil Cream

INGREDIENTS

serves 4

FOCACCIA

620g (1lb 4oz) plain flour

15g (¹/₂ oz) fresh yeast

15ml (¹/₂ fl oz) milk

4 tbsp olive oil

15g (¹/₂ oz) salt

250 ml (9 floz) water

BASIL SAUCE

50g (2oz) potatoes

40g (1¹/₂ oz) basil

250ml (9 floz) vegetable
    stock

15g (¹/₂ oz) spring onions

pinch of salt

TOPPING

2 x 150g (5oz) balls
    buffalo mozzarella

mixed salad leaves

2 red peppers

1 bunch of rosemary

METHOD

1 Place the flour onto a worktop. Dissolve the yeast in lukewarm water then add the milk, the olive oil and the salt. Place the mixed liquid in the middle of the flour and start kneading the dough. Make it into a smooth ball shape, cover with a tea towel and let it rise for 1 hour.

2 Roll the dough out to a thickness of ¹/₂ cm (¹/₄ inch). Cut the dough into 4 circles and place them onto a greased baking tray.

Sprinkle with water, brush with olive oil and place some rosemary and a few crystals of rock salt on top of each. Bake in the oven at 220°C (425°F) for 8-10 minutes, then allow to cool.

3 Meanwhile chop the spring onions and sauté in a pan with a spoonful of butter until golden. Add the thinly sliced potatoes, half the basil, the stock and salt. Let cook for 15 minutes.

4 Once ready, place the mix into a blender and blend with the rest of the basil.

5 Peel the peppers, take out the seeds and cut them into slices. Place them onto a baking tray with salt and pepper and place in a pre-heated oven at 220° C (425°F) until caramelised.

6 Cut the prepared focaccia in half and fill it with 3 slices of mozzarella, 2 spoonfuls of hot basil sauce and a few slices of pepper. Decorate with the salad leaves.

Note: suggested salad leaves include radicchio, rocket and watercress.

Brioche with Peppers, Aubergines & Mozzarella

INGREDIENTS

serves 4-5

500g (1lb) aubergines

500g (1lb) red peppers

400g (16oz) buffalo
   mozzarella, drained
   and cut into slices

150g (5oz) mixed salad
   leaves

150ml (5floz) salad
   dressing

100ml (4floz) olive oil

1 egg, beaten

METHOD

1 *Cut the aubergines into ¹/₂ cm (¹/₄ inch) slices. Season, brush with olive oil and grill lightly.*

2 *Brush red peppers with olive oil, roast in oven pre-heated to 200°C (400°F) for around 20 minutes, cool, peel skin and discard seeds.*

3 *Prepare the brioche dough, and roll out to 20cm x 10cm wide (8 inches x 4 inches). Lay the grilled aubergine in the centre of the dough, leaving a border of about 7cm (3 inches) around the edges.*

4 *Place the peeled red pepper on top of the aubergine and season.*

5 *Put the sliced mozzarella in the centre, being careful not to spread it out too far, so that the mozzarella is surrounded by the aubergine and pepper.*

6 *Then roll up tightly into an oblong sausage shape.*

7 *Lightly coat with egg and bake in a hot oven for 20-25 minutes.*

8 *To serve, cut a slice from the roll and garnish with dressed salad leaves.*

BRIOCHE

500g (1lb)brioche
dough: follow the recipe
on page 154

Crescenta of Mozzarella & Roasted Peppers with Anchoiade

Crescenta

METHOD

1 Knead flour, salt, bicarbonate of soda and milk to a dough, being careful not to overwork it.

2 Wrap the dough in a cloth and leave for 1 hour.

3 Break off small golf-ball-sized pieces of dough and roll out to very thin discs 18cm (7 inches) in diameter.

4 Fry the discs one at a time in plenty of extra virgin olive oil, shaking the pan vigorously until the crescenta airate and become crisp and golden.

5 Drain on kitchen paper, then sprinkle with sea salt and keep warm until ready to serve.

Dressing

METHOD

1 Heat a little olive oil in a small pan. Add shallots and garlic and sweat until soft.

2 Add anchovy fillets, white wine and basil leaves, and bring to the boil.

3 Now blend anchovy mixture with mayonnaise, warm water and the olive oil in a food processor until smooth.

4 Pass through a fine cloth or sieve and season.

Recipe continued overleaf...

INGREDIENTS

Serves 4-6

CRESCENTA

200g (8oz) 'O' Italian flour

pinch of salt

pinch bicarbonate of soda

100ml (4floz) milk

DRESSING

1/2 tin of good anchovy fillets in oil

50g (2oz) shallot, finely chopped

25g (1oz) garlic, finely chopped

75g (3oz) basil leaves

1 large glass white wine

1 tbsp mayonnaise

1 tbsp warm water

30ml (1floz) extra virgin olive oil

TOPPING

serves 4-5

4 x 100g (4oz) balls
buffalo mozzarella

2 large red peppers

12 marinated anchovy
fillets

350g (14 oz) wild rocket
leaves

75g (3oz) shallot rings

100ml (4floz) extra virgin
olive oil

olive oil for frying

sea salt

...continued from previous page

Topping

METHOD

1 *Add a little olive oil to a hot roasting tray.*
2 *When the oil is smoking add peppers and blister all over. Cook in a very hot oven for 2 minutes. Sprinkle with salt.*
3 *Remove from the heat, place in a bowl and cover with cling film.*
4 *Once cool, remove cling film and peel peppers carefully.*
5 *Cut into 12 large strips and sear in a hot, almost dry, pan.*

Assembly

1 *Toss rocket leaves and shallots together in a little oil.*
2 *Cut each ball of mozzarella into 3 thick segments.*
3 *Arrange mozzarella on the crescenta, then also arrange anchovy fillets and roasted pepper strips on the bread.*
4 *Scatter rocket leaves on top and a little sea salt.*
5 *Then spoon the anchovy sauce around and over the crescenta, and finish with a light drizzle of extra virgin olive oil.*

Baked Shallot & Oven Dried Tomato Focaccia with Bocconcini

METHOD

1 *A day in advance, slice tomatoes in half and lay cut side up on tray. Sprinkle with olive oil, salt and black pepper. Place in oven on lowest heat to dry overnight.*

2 *Mix flour, a pinch of salt and the olive oil in a bowl with warm water and mix into a soft, smooth dough for the focaccia. Place in bowl, cover and leave in a warm place for an hour.*

3 *Preheat oven to 200°C (400°F). Heat shallots gently in a small pan with a little olive oil and herbs, then roast in oven until tender, around 15 minutes. Allow to cool in the oil. Brush a baking sheet with some of the oil.*

4 *Cut dough into 4 equal parts and shape into balls, dusting with a little extra flour if necessary. Roll into flat ovals approximately 1¹/₂ cm (¹/₂ inch) thick and lay on the baking sheet.*

5 *Push the shallots into the dough decoratively and drizzle with a little of the shallot oil. Bake for 10 minutes. Add the dried tomatoes to the top and bake again for 4-5 minutes or until the focaccia is golden.*

6 *Place drained bocconcini on top, sprinkle with thyme leaves and bake again for 2-3 minutes or until the cheese just starts to melt.*

7 *Serve while still warm with a salad of mixed leaves tossed in olive oil.*

INGREDIENTS

serves 6

500g (1lb 2oz) cherry tomatoes or very small tomatoes

a little olive oil

rock salt

freshly ground black pepper

12-18 shallots, peeled

1 tsp chopped fresh thyme

1 tsp chopped fresh rosemary

18 bocconcini, drained of excess milk

FOCACCIA

200g (8oz) plain strong flour

4 tbsp olive oil

10g (¹/₄ oz) yeast

a little warm water

Baked Shallot & Oven Dried

Tomato Focaccia with Bocconcini

(recipe on previous page)

Rotolo of Woodroasted Aubergine & Peppers with Brioche

INGREDIENTS

serves 8-10

1 kg (2 lb) roll of buffalo
mozzarella (rotolo),
drained

500 g (1 lb) aubergine

500 g (1 lb) peeled red
peppers

2 bunches green basil

salt & pepper

olive oil

4 tsp fresh basil pesto

1 kg (2 lb) brioche dough
(see recipe page 154)

METHOD

1 Slice the aubergine lengthways, approximately 2cm (1 inch) thick. Rub with olive oil and season with salt and pepper. Lay on a roasting tray and bake in a wood oven (or very hot domestic oven) until brown.

2 Rub the peppers with olive oil and salt and bake as for the aubergine, then allow to cool.

3 Roll the brioche dough out into a rectangle approx. 40cm x 30cm x 1.5cm thick, (20 inches x 15 inches x 1/2 inch) then place in refrigerator and leave.

4 Lay the drained mozzarella onto a sheet of cling film and season, then lay the aubergine flat on top.

5 Pick the basil leaves and cover the aubergine with them, season with salt and pepper, then cover the basil with the roasted peppers.

6 Take care to mop up any excess liquid or juice that may run out.

7 Using the cling film to help, roll the rotolo up like a Swiss roll, making sure it is as tight as possible. Puncture a few holes in the film and leave in refrigerator to chill and drain for 1 hour.

8 Remove the brioche dough from the fridge, unwrap the rotolo and roll up in the brioche dough, then seal the ends.

9 Brush with egg wash and place onto a baking tray. Leave at room temperature for an hour to allow brioche to prove, then bake in medium oven at 170°C (325°F) for 25 minutes.

10 Remove from the oven and leave for 5 minutes before serving. Cut a thick slice and serve with roasted aubergine and a spoonful of fresh pesto.

Note: This dish can be served cold as a picnic item.

Focaccia with Buffalo Mozzarella & Rosemary

METHOD

1 Make the bread recipe outlined below.

2 Preheat the grill or barbecue.

3 Cook dough circles one by one on hot grill for about 2 minutes each side until they bubble and brown.

4 Remove them to a pastry board and while still hot sprinkle with mozzarella that has been turned through a food mill. Lightly sprinkle with salt and pepper, a little rosemary and olive oil. Cut into wedges and devour.

Focaccia

METHOD

1 Mix the warm water, yeast, sugar and half the flour in a mixer with dough hook for 10 minutes until sloppy and foaming.

2 Now add the remaining flour and olive oil gradually.

3 Work the machine for a few further minutes until a sloppy dough is collecting and twisting around the dough hook.

4 Generously oil a bowl. Flour your hands and transfer dough from mixer bowl to the oiled bowl. Slap the dough from side to side, flouring lightly till the oil is absorbed, then lightly oil the top of the dough, turn over and wrap in cling film.

5 Allow to rise to double the size. Remove the cling film and bash down the dough, repeating a few times, then leave for 10-15 minutes.

6 Roll out balls of the dough with your fingertips, to create several very thin circles, approximately 30cm (12 inches) in diameter.

7 Proceed with the rest of the recipe, as above.

INGREDIENTS

serves 4-6

2 x 100g (4oz) balls buffalo mozzarella

black pepper

fresh rosemary

FOCACCIA

1 litre (1^3/$_4$ pints) warm water

25g (1oz) yeast

2 tsp sugar

1.5kg (3 lb) 00 flour

2 tsp salt

3 tbsp olive oil

Polenta, Mozzarella & Parma Ham Sandwich

INGREDIENTS

serves 10-12

500g (1lb) polenta

1500ml (2¹/₂ pints) water

700ml (1¹/₄ pints) milk

700g (1lb 5oz) buffalo
   mozzarella, sliced)

200g (8oz) Parma ham

1 tbsp Dijon mustard

150g (5oz) parmesan cheese

150g (5oz) butter

2 eggs, beaten

200g (8oz) breadcrumbs

25g (1oz) salt

10g (¹/₂ oz) white pepper

METHOD

1 *Bring water, milk and salt to the boil. Slowly whisk in the polenta and bring the mixture back to the boil, whisking constantly.*

2 *Turn the heat down and leave the polenta to bubble slowly for half an hour, whisking occasionally to prevent any lumps forming.*

3 *After about half an hour the polenta should be coming away from the sides of the pan. Remove from the heat and add the butter, parmesan cheese and pepper and mix in well.*

4 *Use a lightly oiled tray and pour a thin layer of polenta into it and spread evenly. Allow to cool. Keep the rest warm.*

5 *When this layer has cooled, spread a thin layer of Dijon mustard over it and arrange the mozzarella to cover the whole area. Slice the Parma ham thinly and layer over the mozzarella.*

6 *Pour over the remaining warm polenta and spread it out thinly to cover the filling. Cool the whole tray for at least an hour.*

7 *When cold, turn out the entire tray in one piece and cut into small neat triangles.*

8 *Coat each piece in flour, then the beaten egg and finally coat with breadcrumbs. Deep fry until crisp and golden brown.*

9 *Serve with parsley salad and a dusting of parmesan.*

Pasta

Simone Cerea / CARAVAGGIO

Fresh Linguine with Asparagus, Sundried Tomatoes & Smoked Mozzarella

Chris Benians / DAPHNE'S

Spaghetti alla Sorrento

Antonello Tagliabue / BICE

Timballo of Aubergines & Orecchiette Pasta with a Mozzarella & Tomato Sauce

Stefan Cavallini / THE HALKIN

Ravioli alla Mozzarella

Theo Randall / RIVER CAFE

Rigatoni with Plum Tomato Sauce, Marjoram, Buffalo Mozzarella & Pecorino

Theo Randall / RIVER CAFE

Baked Buffalo Mozzarella on Pasta Frolla

Lorenzo Berni / SAN LORENZO

Le Penne dei Principi di Paternó

Fresh Linguine with Asparagus, Sundried Tomatoes & Smoked Mozzarella

INGREDIENTS

serves 4

PASTA

100g (4oz) plain flour

100g (4oz) Manitoba flour

1 egg

4 tbsp water

pinch of salt

SAUCE

160g (5oz) fresh asparagus

8 sundried tomatoes

150g (5oz) smoked buffalo
   mozzarella, finely diced

40g (1¹/₂oz) unsalted
   butter

2 tbsp olive oil

20g (³/₄oz) grated
   parmesan

1 small cup of vegetable
   stock

salt & pepper

METHOD

1 To make the pasta, place the 2 types of flour in a mixing bowl. Mix the egg and water together and fold into the flour until the mixture reaches an elastic and dough-like consistency. Leave to stand for 2 hours. Break into 4 portions and roll each into a thin sheet. Cut into thin strips and sprinkle with flour to prevent from sticking together.

2 For the sauce, cut the asparagus into cubes and boil for 2 minutes. Melt half the butter with half of the olive oil. Add the asparagus and sundried tomatoes and lightly fry. Add stock and simmer for 5 minutes.

3 Place pasta in a pan of boiling salted water for 3-4 minutes, stirring occasionally. Strain off the water and add the asparagus, tomatoes and stock. Add the remainder of the butter, olive oil and parmesan. Gently mix together until it reaches a smooth and creamy consistency and serve on 4 small heated plates, topped with finely diced mozzarella.

Spaghetti
alla Sorrento

INGREDIENTS

serves 4

250g (10oz) spaghetti

8 plum tomatoes

2 x 100g (4oz) balls
  buffalo mozzarella

half bunch basil

3 tbsp very good quality
  olive oil

rock salt

black pepper

METHOD

1 *Place the spaghetti to
cook in a large pan of well
salted boiling water.*

2 *Meanwhile cube the
tomatoes and mozzarella
and place into a bowl with
the olive oil. Season with
salt and pepper. Tear the
basil leaves and scatter in.*

3 *When the spaghetti is
al dente, drain and place
into the bowl with the other
ingredients, toss and serve.*

*Note: This dish is so simple
that all the ingredients must
be of the highest quality.
Since the 'sauce' is raw,
the end dish is purposely
warm rather than hot
and is intended for a light
summer's lunch.*

INGREDIENTS

serves 1

7 slices aubergine

25g (1oz) buffalo
  mozzarella, diced except
  for 1 slice

50g (2oz) orecchiette
  pasta

50g (2oz) fresh tomato
  sauce (see recipe on
  page 155)

5 basil leaves

1 tbsp grated parmesan

50g (2oz) breadcrumbs

1 egg, beaten

250ml (10floz) of pre-
  ferred oil for frying

salt & pepper

Timballo of Aubergines & Orecchiette Pasta with a Mozzarella & Tomato Sauce

METHOD

1 Place the aubergine slices on a tea towel, sprinkle them with salt and let the water evaporate for about 10 minutes before drying them well.

2 Dip the slices in egg and then roll them in the breadcrumbs. Fry them and lay on paper towels to absorb any excess oil. Line a baking tin with some foil and place a layer of aubergines on the bottom.

3 Cook the pasta al dente. Meanwhile heat the tomato sauce and add some basil leaves. Drain the pasta and then sauté together with the tomato sauce. Then add the diced mozzarella (reserving a slice for decoration) and some grated parmesan.

4 Place the pasta in the baking tray, wrap the aubergine extremities around the pasta and place in a preheated oven at 180°C (350°F) for 5 minutes, until the mozzarella melts.

5 Turn the timballo onto a plate, garnish with a spoonful of tomato sauce, a basil leaf and a mozzarella slice.

Ravioli alla Mozzarella

METHOD

1 Clean the artichokes in advance.

2 Heat a little bit of olive oil in a heavy based saucepan, sauté the garlic and thyme, then add the artichokes and white wine and cover.

3 Simmer until the wine is reduced, then add the vegetable stock and cover again. When cooked, let them cool.

4 Remove the artichokes from the pan and dice. Cut the mozzarella into cubes. Place both ingredients in a bowl and add the basil, salt and pepper.

5 Cut the pasta sheets into 40 x 4cm (2 inch) squares. On top of 20 squares place equal mounds of the artichoke and mozzarella mixture, then cover with the remaining 20 squares, pressing around the edges to make small parcels.

6 Cook the ravioli in a large pot of boiling salted water.

7 Meanwhile chop the 4 tomatoes and sauté with a little olive oil. In a separate pan, melt the butter.

8 Remove the ravioli from the water and drain. Arrange 5 ravioli on each plate and top with a few spoonfuls of the sautéed tomato. To serve, sprinkle with the pine kernels and parmesan, and drizzle over the melted butter.

INGREDIENTS

serves 4

4 artichokes

3 x 100g (4oz) balls buffalo mozzarella

4 tomatoes

3 basil leaves, finely chopped

100g (4oz) ravioli pasta sheets

2 tbsp extra virgin olive oil

1 sprig thyme

100ml (4floz) of white wine

100ml (4floz) of vegetable stock

2 cloves garlic

20g (^{1}/$_2$oz) pine kernels

60g (2oz) butter

20g (^{1}/$_2$oz) parmesan

salt & pepper

Rigatoni with Plum Tomato Sauce, Marjoram, Buffalo Mozzarella & Pecorino

INGREDIENTS

serves 4

2 cloves garlic

1 bunch fresh marjoram
leaves

2 tins Italian peeled plum
tomatoes

4 tbsp extra virgin olive oil

2 x 125g (4$^{1}/_{2}$ oz) balls
buffalo mozzarella, cut
into small pieces

100g (4oz) pecorino
cheese, or reggiano
parmesan

500g (1lb) rigatoni pasta

METHOD

1 *Slice garlic very thinly and fry gently in olive oil until a light golden colour.*
2 *Add marjoram leaves and cook for a few seconds. Reduce to low heat and add the plum tomatoes. Cook slowly for 40 minutes or until the mixture reaches a thick consistency.*
3 *In a large saucepan bring to the boil 2 litres (4 pints) of salted water, add rigatoni and cook until al dente. Drain pasta, add tomato sauce, fold in mozzarella, pecorino, season and serve.*

Baked Buffalo Mozzarella on Pasta Frolla

METHOD

1 Place all the pasta ingredients into a food processor and pulse until a dough forms. Wrap the dough in cling film and chill for a minimum of 45 minutes. This can be done 24 hours in advance.

2 Roll out dough on a flat surface to 20cm by 40cm (10 inches x 20 inches). Chill in refrigerator for a further 30 minutes. Remove dough from refrigerator, and cut into 6 equal squares. Bake on a pastry sheet at 180°C

(350°F) for 15 minutes, or until golden brown. Set aside to cool.

3 Preheat oven to 240°C (450°F). Cut each mozzarella ball into 4 slices and place on each slice of pastry. Slice potatoes wafer thin (if possible use mandolin, or slicer on food processor; alternatively, blanch potatoes, and slice as thinly as possible by hand).

4 Layer potato slices on top of mozzarella, with garlic, thyme, grated parmesan, and generous amounts of

black pepper. Bake in oven for 8-10 minutes, until mozzarella begins to melt and parmesan goldens.

5 If available, serve covered with thinly sliced white truffles. Otherwise, drizzle with good quality truffle oil.

Note: White truffles are in season between mid October and late December but are hard to come by, as well as expensive, and can probably only be used as an exceptional treat. Truffle oil is a good substitute.

INGREDIENTS

serves 6

PASTA FROLLA

125g (4$\frac{1}{2}$oz) unsalted
   butter

200g (8oz) plain flour

4 tbsp iced water

pinch salt

TOPPING

6 x 125g (4$\frac{1}{2}$oz) balls
   buffalo mozzarella

4 waxy potatoes, Charlotte
   or Roseval, peeled

4 sprigs of thyme, leaves
   picked and washed

2 cloves garlic, finely
   sliced

100g (4oz) grated
   parmesan

black pepper

60g (2oz) white truffles
   (optional)

Le Penne dei Principi di Paternó

INGREDIENTS

serves 4

250g (10oz) peeled
   tomatoes

1 onion, chopped

1 clove garlic, chopped

2 cloves garlic, whole

6 tbsp olive oil

500g (1 lb) penne pasta

100g (4oz) black olives

200g (8oz) buffalo
   mozzarella

2 tbsp coarse rock salt

black pepper

a few basil leaves

METHOD

1 *Begin by preparing a basic tomato sauce: Heat 3 tbsp of the olive oil in a frying pan and sauté the chopped onions with chopped garlic until golden.*

2 *Then add the peeled the tomatoes and salt and pepper to taste. Add the two whole garlic cloves. Cook for about 20 minutes until the excess liquid evaporates, then remove the two garlic cloves. (Add 1 tsp of tomato paste to enrich the taste if desired.)*

3 *Bring a saucepan of water to the boil, and add 2 large tbsp of coarse rock salt.*

4 *Add the penne to the boiling water and cook until al dente.*

5 *While the pasta is cooking, cut the mozzarella into small cubes.*

6 *When the pasta is ready, drain and place into a serving bowl, add the tomato sauce, the olives and mozzarella. Mix through gently. Drizzle over the remaining spoonfuls of olive oil, using*

more or less as preferred.

7 *Serve immediately, garnishing with a few fresh basil leaves on top.*

Note: It is important that the mozzarella is added at the last moment when the pasta has cooled a fraction, to prevent the cheese from melting too much and becoming stringy.

Legumi

David Burke / LE PONT DE LA TOUR
Ballotine of Grilled Vegetables with Buffalo Mozzarella

Alberto Chiappa / MONTPELIANO
Mozzarella, Asparagus, Raisins & Pine Nuts with Vinaigrette al Peperone

Paul Wilson / GEORGES
Seared Tomatoes with Caponata & Mozzarella

Chris Benians, DAPHNE'S
Buffalo Mozzarella with Rolled Aubergine & Pesto

Chris Benians / DAPHNE'S
Buffalo Mozzarella with Peppers Piedmontese

Henrik Iversen / QUAGLINO'S
Buffalo Mozzarella with Couscous, Lemon, Parsley & Capers

Alastair Little / ALASTAIR LITTLE
Gâteau of Grilled Vegetables & Mozzarella

Matthew Harris / BIBENDUM
Fried Mozzarella with Anchovy Dressing, French Bean Salad & Parmesan

Stefan Cavallini / THE HALKIN
Fiori di Zucchina

Sally Clarke / CLARKE'S
Grilled Finger Aubergine with Purple Basil & Mozzarella

Alberico Penati / ANNABEL'S
Smoked Buffalo Mozzarella with Porcini Mushrooms

Simon Arkless / OXO TOWER
Baked Tomatoes with Basil Cream & Melted Mozzarella on Herb Crostini

Henrik Iversen / QUAGLINO'S
Aubergine & Buffalo Mozzarella Beignet with Salsify & Balsamic

Alberico Penati / HARRY'S BAR
Sculpted Vegetables with Bocconcini

Alberico Penati / HARRY'S BAR
Bean Pâtè & Buffalo Mozzarella with Vegetable Mayonnaise

Simon Arkless / OXO TOWER
Grilled Flat Mushrooms with Melted Mozzarella & Sundried Pepper & Pickled Chilli Relish

David Burke / LE PONT DE LA TOUR
Buffalo Mozzarella, Tomato & Pesto Tart

Ballotine of Grilled Vegetables with Buffalo Mozzarella

INGREDIENTS

serves 4

3 aubergines

6 courgettes

3 red peppers

2 x 100g (4oz) buffalo
  mozzarella

100g (4oz) pesto

salt & pepper

400g (16oz) gazpacho
  (optional)

METHOD

1 Roast the peppers in a hot oven for 10 minutes until blistered. Remove from the oven and let them cool down. Peel off the skin, split in half and deseed. Then grill on both sides for 2 minutes.

2 Slice the aubergines and courgettes very thinly, preferably on a mandolin. Season the slices, brush with oil, and grill on both sides for 2 minutes. Remove from the heat and let cool.

3 Lay a sheet of cling film on a flat surface, place the aubergine on top widthways and brush lightly with some pesto.

4 Next place a layer of courgettes on top of the aubergines.

5 Using the cling film as an aid, start to roll the layered vegetables as if making a swiss roll. Continue to roll very tightly until you have a cylindrical shape. Tie both ends of the ballotine tightly and refrigerate for 30 minutes.

6 Remove cling film and cut into 12 even slices. Divide equally among 4 plates with 3 slices of mozzarella on each. Finish with a little cracked pepper and gazpacho if desired.

INGREDIENTS

serves 4

4 x 100g (4oz) balls
  buffalo mozzarella

12 asparagus spears

1 garlic clove

2 tbsp olive oil

1 spring onion

1 tsp balsamic vinegar

salt & pepper

basil

50g (2oz) sultanas

50g (2oz) pine nuts

VINAIGRETTE

2 red peppers

1 garlic clove

4 tbsp olive oil

2 shallots

salt & pepper

1 tsp french mustard

1 tsp tomato paste

Mozzarella, Asparagus, Raisins & Pine Nuts with Vinaigrette al Peperone

METHOD

1 Soak the sultanas in water for 15 minutes. Meanwhile boil the asparagus in salted water for 2-3 minutes and then quickly cool the spears in cold water. Cut them in half and then into 2cm (1 inch) pieces.

2 Gently fry 1 garlic clove, still in its skin, in oil. Add the coarsely chopped spring onion to the garlic, frying for another 2 minutes.

3 Remove the garlic, and add the pine nuts, frying them slightly. Drain the sultanas and pat dry on kitchen paper. Add to the spring onions and pine nuts.

4 Add the asparagus, salt and freshly ground pepper. Flash cook for 2 minutes, remove from heat and allow to cool.

5 Grill the peppers on a hot grill for about 15-20 minutes. Remove and place on a dish, covering with cling film for a few minutes so the skin comes off easily.

6 Skin the peppers and remove the seeds. Coarsely chop the flesh and set aside. Fry the shallots and 1 garlic clove for 2-3 minutes.

7 Remove the garlic, add the peppers, salt and pepper, mustard and tomato paste. Cook slowly for 5 minutes and add 3 tbsp of water.

8 Place in a liquidizer and then pass through a small sieve, whisking gently with a fork and adding the last 2 tbsp of olive oil. Cut each mozzarella ball into 6 slices and place in a circle in a round dish so they overlap slightly, and place the asparagus in the centre.

9 Garnish with the basil leaves and spoon over the vinaigrette.

Seared Tomatoes with Caponata & Mozzarella

INGREDIENTS

serves 4

500g (1lb) plum tomatoes
blanched and peeled

425g (17oz) buffalo
mozzarella

25g (1oz) flat-leaf parsley

150g (5oz) basil leaves

30g (1oz) shallot rings

3 tbsp extra virgin olive oil

3 tbsp balsamic vinegar

6 cloves garlic, crushed

juice of 1 lemon

sea salt & milled pepper

Caponata

1 *Salt aubergines and allow to drain for 15 minutes.*

2 *In a large casserole gently heat some of the olive oil and fry the celery with leaves until soft (around 10 minutes).*

3 *Add garlic and aubergines and stew gently for 30 minutes. Season, add tomato purée and cook gently.*

4 *Mix vinegar and sugar together in a separate pan, bring to the boil and taste. The mixture should have a pleasant sweet and sour taste; if not add more sugar or vinegar depending on your preference.*

5 *Add this to the aubergine mix and cook for a further hour until everything is well stewed like a compote.*

6 *Then add olives, capers and the basil, reserving a few capers for the final garnish. Check seasoning and allow to cool.*

Seared Tomatoes

1 *Crush garlic with a little salt and lemon.*

2 *Add most of the olive oil and mix in the vinegar.*

3 *Season and add basil, then set aside the marinade.*

4 *Heat a little olive oil in a very hot pan until oil is smoking.*

5 *Carefully add tomatoes, 2-3 at a time, and sear well on all sides.*

6 *Season whilst warm and place into the marinade for at least an hour or more.*

7 *Place a generous spoonful of the room temperature caponata in the centre of each plate and spread out evenly.*

8 *Place 2 seared tomatoes on the caponata. Place several thick slices of buffalo mozzarella next to the tomatoes. Season with salt and milled pepper.*

9 *Toss basil, parsley and shallot rings in some of the extra virgin olive oil and arrange on top of the tomatoes and mozzarella.*

10 *Lastly, sprinkle on a few capers and drizzle over the remaining olive oil and balsamic vinegar.*

CAPONATA

500g (1 lb) green pitted
 olives
500g (1 lb) aubergines,
 diced into 2cm (1 inch)
 segments
500g (1 lb) onions,
 diced into 2cm (1 inch)
 segments
500g (1 lb) celery with
 leaves, diced into 2cm
 (1 inch) segments
3 tbsp red wine vinegar
300ml (12floz) olive oil
3 cloves garlic
3 tbsp balsamic vinegar
90g (3oz) sugar
60g (2oz) tomato purée
120g (4¹/₂oz) basil
60g (2oz) capers

Buffalo Mozzarella with Rolled Aubergine & Pesto

METHOD

1 Thinly slice the aubergines lengthways into strips so that you have at least 12 slices in total. Lightly oil the slices and chargrill on both sides until cooked, then place on a tray and brush with balsamic vinegar and leave to cool.

2 Prepare the filling by mixing together the capers, tomatoes, olives, parsley and vinegar. Place a heaped teaspoon of filling on each slice of aubergine and roll it up.

3 To make the pesto, blend the basil, pine nuts, garlic and olive oil together using either a pestle and mortar or a food processor.

4 Slice each ball of mozzarella into 6 pieces and place 3 onto each plate. Then place 3 of the aubergine rolls next to that and spoon some of the pesto around. Garnish with some fresh whole basil leaves.

INGREDIENTS

serves 2

2 x 100g (4oz) balls
  buffalo mozzarella

2 aubergines

2 tbsp salted baby capers

2 tbsp chopped tomatoes

1 tbsp chopped black olives

1 tbsp chopped parsley

1 tbsp balsamic vinegar

50g (2oz) fresh basil

25g (1oz) pine nuts

3 cloves garlic, peeled

200ml (8floz) olive oil

Buffalo Mozzarella with Peppers Piedmontese

INGREDIENTS

serves 2

2 x 100g (4oz) balls
  buffalo mozzarella

2 red peppers

2 yellow peppers

4 plum tomatoes

8 salted anchovy fillets
  (optional)

4 basil leaves

1 tbsp olive oil

METHOD

1 *Cut the peppers in half lengthways through the core, leaving it attached, and trim out the seeds. Season the insides of the peppers with salt, pepper, a slice of garlic, a whole basil leaf, and an anchovy fillet.*

2 *Cut the tomatoes in half and place equal portions into the middle of each pepper. Then season again and drizzle with olive oil.*

3 *Place into an oiled, thick-based ovenproof dish, cover with foil and bake in a moderate oven for 1 hour.*

4 *After 1 hour remove the foil and continue to cook the peppers for another 30 minutes. By this time the peppers should be very soft and the tomatoes slightly shrivelled. Leave the peppers to cool, then serve with several slices of mozzarella.*

Buffalo Mozzarella with Couscous, Lemon, Parsley & Capers

METHOD

1 To make the couscous salad, mix the couscous with the cucumber, $^1/_4$ of the olive oil, $^3/_4$ of the tomato, $^1/_2$ of the lemon juice, $^1/_2$ of the chopped parsley, and $^3/_4$ of the red onion. Season with salt and pepper.

2 Set aside the salad while you make the dressing, mixing together the remaining parsley, lemon juice and zest, diced tomato, capers, shallots, and olive oil. Season with salt and pepper.

3 Divide the couscous salad into 4 portions and press into a circular patty on each serving plate.

4 Slice the mozzarella and arrange neatly on top.

5 Spoon some of the dressing over each plate, partially covering the mozzarella.

INGREDIENTS

serves 4

2 x 100g (4oz) balls
   buffalo mozzarella, sliced

250g (10oz) couscous,
   cooked

2 plum tomatoes, peeled,
   deseeded and diced

25g (1oz) shallot rings

$^1/_4$ cucumber, peeled
   and diced

$^1/_2$ red onion, diced

50g (2oz) chopped parsley

grated zest and juice of
   1 lemon

30g (1oz) capers

250ml (10floz) virgin
   olive oil

30g (1oz) shaved parmesan

salt & pepper

Gâteau of Grilled Vegetables & Mozzarella

METHOD

1 *Preheat oven to 170°C (325°F).*

2 *Scorch the peppers over a direct flame until blackened all over. Allow to cool a little, then peel quickly under running water over a colander. Pat dry, open out, remove seeds and cut the flesh into 4cm (2 inch) squares. Lay on a plate and season with salt, pepper and olive oil.*

3 *Cut the aubergines into 8 x 1cm ($^1/_2$ inch) slices. Season and oil generously on both sides. Put on a baking sheet in a single layer and bake until collapsed and tender (around 15-20 minutes). Remove from baking sheet and transfer to a large plate or tray.*

4 *Skin the tomatoes and slice into 8 x $^1/_2$ cm ($^1/_4$ inch) slices, then lay them out on another large plate.*

5 *Slice the mozzarella into 12 slices. Leave in a sieve to drain. Pick basil leaves.*

6 *Take 4 plates. Put 1 slice of aubergine on each plate. Lay a slice of mozzarella on top, then a slice of tomato and 1 basil leaf. Follow this with a piece of pepper, then mozzarella, then tomato and basil, and another aubergine slice to finish.*

7 *Before serving, drizzle oil on top and scatter with torn basil leaves and chopped pitted olives (optional).*

Note: It is important that all the vegetables are correctly seasoned before assembly, and that the mozzarella is well drained.

INGREDIENTS

serves 4

2 x 100g (4oz) balls
   buffalo mozzarella

2 aubergines

1 red pepper

1 yellow pepper

2 large ripe tomatoes

16 basil leaves

good quality olive oil

salt & pepper

handful of pitted olives
   (optional)

Fried Mozzarella with Anchovy Dressing, French Bean Salad & Parmesan

METHOD

1 To make the dressing blend the first 5 ingredients in a food processor until smooth and then add the oil in a thin stream whilst still blending (as if you were making mayonnaise). When finished, season with pepper. If the dressing seems too thick, add a little water to thin it until it reaches the consistency of double cream. The dressing will keep in the fridge for 3 or 4 days.

2 Cook the beans in plenty of salted boiling water. When they are just cooked take them out and run them under the cold tap until cool.

3 Now the mozzarella has to be breadcrumbed. To do this you need 3 bowls, 1 containing the plain flour, 1 with the beaten egg and 1 with the breadcrumbs. You then cut each ball of mozzarella into 3 slices. Dip 1 slice of mozzarella at a time into the flour, making sure every inch is covered. Then dip into the egg, again making sure every bit is covered. Then dip into the breadcrumbs. When all the mozzarella slices have been coated in breadcrumbs, place them on a tray making sure the pieces do not touch each other. They are now ready to cook when you want.

4 When almost ready to serve, put the French beans in a bowl and dress with a little bit of olive oil, chopped shallots and salt and pepper. Divide the beans among 4 plates.

5 Heat up a deep fryer, or oil in a frypan, and fry the prepared mozzarella slices. Do not overcrowd the fryer. You can do a few pieces at a time and then keep them warm on a rack in the oven until they are all done.

6 When the mozzarella is done, place several slices on each mound of beans. Drizzle generously with the anchovy dressing, sprinkle with parmesan and serve.

INGREDIENTS

serves 4

4 x 100g (4oz) balls
  buffalo mozzarella

400g (16oz) French beans,
  trimmed

3 shallots, finely chopped

30g (1oz) grated parmesan

250g (10oz) flour

2 eggs, beaten

250g (10oz) breadcrumbs

1 tbsp olive oil

vegetable oil for frying

ANCHOVY DRESSING

1 small tin of anchovies
  in oil

3 tsp capers

1 clove garlic

juice of 1 lemon

3 egg yolks

400ml (16floz) olive oil

pepper

Fiori di Zucchina

INGREDIENTS

serves 4

8 large courgette flowers
   with courgettes attached

1 x 200g (8oz) ball
   buffalo mozzarella

2 anchovies

1 tomato, finely chopped

2 basil leaves

30g (1oz) sweet and sour
   sauce

500ml (18floz) vegetable
   oil

300g (12oz) flour

1 pinch bicarbonate of soda

150ml (5floz) cold water

salt & pepper

2 tbsp extra virgin olive oil

METHOD

1 Remove the flowers from the courgettes and scoop out their fleshy insides. Slice the courgettes and put aside.

2 Cut the mozzarella into cubes and place in a mixing bowl. Add half of the chopped tomato. Chop the anchovies and basil and add these together with salt and pepper to season.

3 Gently open each of the flowers and fill with equal portions of the mozzarella mixture.

4 In a bowl, mix the flour with the bicarbonate. Add the cold water and whisk until a paste forms. Then set aside in the refrigerator.

5 In a shallow pan warm the sweet and sour sauce and add the rest of the tomato. This should stay on a low heat to gradually warm while the next stages are prepared.

6 Heat the extra virgin olive oil and sauté the courgettes. Drain and divide among 4 plates.

7 Now deep fry the courgette flowers, heating the vegetable oil to around 170°C (325°F). When lightly golden, remove from oil and drain. Cut in half and place on top of the bed of courgettes. Spoon the heated sauce around the plate.

Grilled Finger Aubergine

with Purple Basil & Mozzarella

(recipe on following page)

INGREDIENTS

serves 6

6 small to medium
  finger aubergines

8 tbsp olive oil

rock salt

freshly ground black
  pepper

2 bunches of purple basil
  (or green if unavailable),
  leaves picked and
  chopped

6 x 200g (8oz) balls
  buffalo mozzarella,
  drained of excess milk

12 tbsp fresh breadcrumbs,
  fried in a little olive oil
  until crisp, and seasoned
  with salt & pepper

Grilled Finger Aubergine with Purple Basil & Mozzarella

METHOD

1 *Preheat chargrill to highest setting or heat oven to 200°C (400°F)*

2 *Slice aubergines in half lengthways and drizzle half the olive oil over the slices. If using a chargrill, cook until the bar marks are clearly defined on the aubergines, criss-crossing if desired. Season with salt and pepper and half the purple basil. If using an oven, place aubergine halves on a baking sheet, season with salt, pepper and half the chopped purple basil and roast in oven until almost tender (about 10 minutes).*

3 *Cut balls of mozzarella in halves or quarters, season with salt and pepper and arrange with aubergines on serving plates, drizzled with the remaining olive oil.*

4 *To serve, mix the remaining basil with the toasted breadcrumbs and sprinkle on top of the aubergines.*

INGREDIENTS

serves 4

250g (10oz) red onions,
  cut into rings

8 small, whole porcini
  mushrooms

4 x 100g (4oz) slices of
  smoked buffalo mozzarella

1 bay leaf

1 sprig rosemary

salt and pepper

100ml (4oz) extra virgin
  olive oil

4 tbsp balsamic
  vinegar

Smoked Buffalo Mozzarella with Porcini Mushrooms

METHOD

1 *Brown the onions in 50ml (2floz) of olive oil until they are just translucent.*

2 *Lightly cook the mushrooms with the bay leaf,* *rosemary and the rest of the oil. Add salt and pepper.*

3 *In a hot, nonstick pan, grill the mozzarella slices quickly on either side before they begin to melt.*

4 *On each of 4 serving plates, layer a base of red onions, a mozzarella slice, and the mushrooms and herbs. Sprinkle with the balsamic vinegar.*

Baked Tomatoes with Basil Cream & Melted Mozzarella on Herb Crostini

INGREDIENTS

serves 4

300ml (12floz) double
  cream

100ml (4floz) creme
  fraiche

2 garlic cloves, peeled and
  crushed

6 large ripe plum tomatoes,
  cut in half lengthways
  and deseeded.

salt & black pepper

1 small bunch of basil

200g (8oz) buffalo
  mozzarella

4 slices of french country
  bread, toasted and
  rubbed with garlic and
  olive oil

1 tbsp chopped mixed
  herbs (tarragon, parsley,
  chervil, basil)

2 tsp grated parmesan

1 tsp sugar

METHOD

1 *Place the tomatoes (cut side uppermost) in an oven-proof dish with a little olive oil. Season and place in a preheated oven at 190°C (375°F) for 10 minutes.*

2 *While the tomatoes cook, put the cream, creme fraiche, garlic, basil stalks and sugar into a pan and simmer until reduced by a third. Add the roughly chopped basil, then pour this mixture over the tomatoes and cook in the oven for a further 15 minutes. The cream should have thick-ened and taken on a slightly pink hue from the tomatoes.*

3 *Meanwhile sprinkle the chopped herbs on top of the toasted bread and slice the mozzarella.*

4 *When the tomatoes are cooked, remove them from the cream, place 3 halves on each piece of toast, sprinkle with a little parme-san and finish with a slice of mozzarella.*

5 *Place on a baking tray and cook for a further 5 minutes until the cheese begins to melt, remove from the oven and place on a warm plate. Pour around the reduced basil cream and complete with a generous twist of black pepper.*

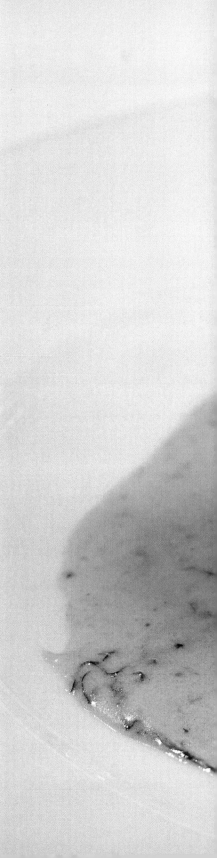

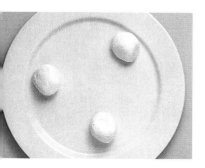

Aubergine & Buffalo Mozzarella Beignet with Salsify & Balsamic

INGREDIENTS

serves 4

3 x 150g (5oz) balls buffalo
mozzarella, halved

100g (4oz) pesto

2 medium aubergines

2 sticks scrubbed salsify

16 cherry tomatoes

250g (10oz) plain flour

2 eggs, beaten

200ml (8floz) dark beer

16 green basil leaves

salt & pepper

40g (1oz) shaved parmesan

oil for frying

1 tbsp 12 year old balsamic

METHOD

1 *In advance, pierce the cherry tomatoes and lay in a baking tray on a bed of rock salt and roast at 120°C (250°F) for an hour.*

2 *Meanwhile prepare the batter, mixing together the beer, eggs, and half the flour. Whisk together, then strain through a sieve and season.*

3 *Cut the aubergines into 12 even slices, season each slice and spread with pesto.*

4 *Place half a mozzarella ball on each of 6 slices, then top with another slice of aubergine, pesto side down to make a sandwich. Mix the remaining pesto into the beer batter.*

5 *Coat each sandwich evenly in flour, shaking off any excess, then dip into the batter. Fry in a deep fat fryer at 150°C (300°F), or in a saucepan over medium-high heat in about 4 inches of oil. When golden brown, remove, drain and season.*

6 *Cut the salsify in fine long ribbons. In a warm saucepan heat the olive oil, then add the salsify, season, and cook for 2-3 minutes. Add the balsamic, basil leaves and tomatoes. Remove from heat and use straightaway.*

7 *To serve, cut each beignet in half and place 3 halves, cut side down on each of 4 plates. Arrange the salsify, tomato and basil neatly on each plate, then spoon over the remaining balsamic and olive oil.*

Sculpted Vegetables with Bocconcini

METHOD

1 *Wash and trim the courgettes and daikon, and cook each separately in salted water. Boil the turnips in salted water adding the saffron towards the end for just a few seconds.*

2 *Cut the tomatoes into cylinders, and sculpt the cooked vegetables into shapes as desired.*

3 *For the dressing, mix the olive oil and lemon juice with the nutmeg, crushed coriander and cloves.*

4 *Arrange the vegetables and mozzarella on 4 serving plates and drizzle over the dressing.*

INGREDIENTS

serves 4

2 large beetroot, bought
   already cooked

4 tomatoes

4 turnips

4 baby courgettes

4 daikon (Japanese radish)

100g (4fl oz) extra virgin
   olive oil

juice of 1 lemon

nutmeg, coriander

5 cloves

16 mozzarella bocconcini

Bean Pâté with Buffalo Mozzarella & Vegetable Mayonnaise

INGREDIENTS

serves 4

300g (12oz) white canellini
   beans, cooked

200g (8oz) buffalo
   mozzarella treccine,
   cut into 4 pieces

50g (2oz) ricotta cheese

70ml (3floz) olive oil

finely chopped herbs

**VEGETABLE
MAYONNAISE**

200g (8oz) steamed
   vegetables (green beans,
   spinach and courgettes)

150ml (5floz) extra virgin
   olive oil

METHOD

*1 To make the pâté,
place half the cooked beans
together with the ricotta
cheese into a food processor,
blend on maximum for
20 seconds, and then strain
through a sieve. Whip the
mixture together with 50ml
(2floz) olive oil. Season
with salt and pepper.*

*2 To make the vegetable
mayonnaise, blend the vegetables and oil on maximum
speed for a maximum of
20 seconds.*

*3 To serve, arrange the pâté
at the bottom of each plate.
Arrange the rest of the
beans on the other side
of the plate and dress with
the herbs and oil. Arrange
the mozzarella on top of
this with a pinch of salt and
spoon over the mayonnaise.
Decorate with fresh herbs.*

Grilled Flat Mushrooms & Melted Mozzarella with Sundried Pepper & Pickled Chilli Relish

INGREDIENTS

serves 4

4 very large flat
   mushrooms approx 12 cm
   (5 inches) in diameter

200g (8oz) buffalo
   mozzarella

4 tbsp of pine nuts,
   lightly toasted

90g (3¹/₂oz) sundried
   peppers

60g (2oz) Spanish pickled
   chillies

1 clove crushed garlic

1 small bunch fresh basil

25ml (1floz) of good
   quality balsamic vinegar

50ml (2floz) extra virgin
   olive oil

2 tbsp grated parmesan

salt & pepper

METHOD

1 Prepare the relish in advance. Thinly slice the sundried peppers and then cover with a little boiling water to reconstitute for about 20 minutes. Pour off excess water. Thinly slice the pickled chillies discarding the stalks. (Pickled chillies come in varying degrees of strength; if the chillies are too hot for you, discard the seeds from the middle before slicing).

2 In a bowl mix the peppers, chillies, garlic, pine nuts, fresh basil (finely chopped), balsamic vinegar and olive oil. Season to taste and the relish is ready.

3 Next, peel the mushrooms and remove the stalks. Brush with a little olive oil, season and cook under a hot grill or in a hot oven on a baking tray for 6-8 minutes.

4 Slice the mozzarella into 1cm (¹/₂ inch) pieces and spread on top of the mushrooms. Season the mozzarella and sprinkle a little parmesan on top.

Return to the grill or oven until the cheese melts and is a light golden brown on top.

5 Remove from the grill and serve on a warm plate. Spoon the relish around and serve immediately.

Note: Sundried peppers may be hard to obtain; if so fresh red peppers can be used. Just deseed, thinly slice and sauté in a frying pan with olive oil and salt and pepper until the peppers are soft.

Buffalo Mozzarella, Tomato & Pesto Tart

METHOD

1 Preheat the oven to 190°C (375°F).

2 Roll out the pastry to a thickness of 3mm, or $^1/_8$ of an inch.

3 Using a round pastry cutter, cut four discs of about 12.5cm, or 5 inches, in diameter. Prick the centre of each disc with a fork.

4 On each pastry disc place alternate slices of mozzarella and tomato, then top with a teaspoon of pesto. Refrigerate for 15 minutes.

5 Then remove from fridge and brush a little of the beaten egg on the edge of each disc. Place on a tray, lined with baking paper, and put in the oven. Cook for 15-20 minutes until the pastry is crisp and golden.

6 Remove from oven and serve, drizzling a little of the basil-flavoured olive oil on each tart.

INGREDIENTS

serves 4

550g (1lb 2oz) puff pastry

4-6 large plum tomatoes, blanched, sliced

2 x 100g (4oz) balls buffalo mozzarella, sliced

100g (4oz) pesto

2 eggs, beaten

2 tbsp basil-flavoured olive oil (or substitute shredded basil in olive oil)

Riso e Risotto

Simon Arkless / OXO TOWER
Butternut Squash, Mozzarella & Caramelised Garlic Risotto with Crispy Shallots & Pesto

Alberto Chiappa / MONTPELIANO
Risotto Mantecato

Henry Harris / FIFTH FLOOR, HARVEY NICHOLS
Spiced Tomato & Mozzarella Risotto

Matthew Harris / BIBENDUM
Saffron & Mozzarella Risotto with Rocket

Alberico Penati / ANNABEL'S
Red Onions & Buffalo Mozzarella on a Bed of Wild Rice

Dean Carr / THE AVENUE
Mozzarella, Basil & Tomato Risotto

Theo Randall / RIVER CAFE
Risotto with Pancetta Affumicata, Buffalo Mozzarella & Savoy Cabbage

Butternut Squash, Mozzarella & Caramelised Garlic Risotto with Crispy Shallots & Pesto

INGREDIENTS

serves 4

400g (16oz) Arborio rice

75g (3oz) unsalted butter

1.6 litres (2^1/$_3$ pints) chicken stock (hot)

1 small onion, finely sliced

50g (2oz) freshly grated parmesan

400g (16oz) butternut squash

125g (4^1/$_2$oz) buffalo mozzarella, diced into 1cm (^{1}/$_2$inch) cubes

16 cloves garlic, peeled

50g (2oz) peeled shallot, finely sliced

100g (4oz) seasoned flour

vegetable oil for frying

PESTO

1 large bunch basil

3 garlic cloves

3 tbsp pine kernels lightly toasted

3 tbsp grated parmesan

olive oil

METHOD

1 First make the pesto. Put garlic, basil and pine kernels in a food processor with a little salt and pepper. Work to a paste then add enough olive oil to produce a loose-textured purèe. Remove from the food processor, pour into a bowl and fold in the parmesan.

2 Next, dust the shallots in seasoned flour, shake off any excess and deep fry in vegetable oil at 160°C (300°F). When a light golden brown, remove from the oil, shake off excess and place on kitchen paper. Season with a little salt and keep ready on a warm plate.

3 To caramelise the garlic, first blanch the garlic in a pan of salted boiling water for about 3 minutes, then transfer to a clean pan, pour off water and add 200ml (8floz) of chicken stock and a knob of butter. Cook till the garlic is soft and the stock is reduced down to a syrup that will coat the garlic cloves.

4 Peel and deseed the butternut squash, dice into 1cm (^{1}/$_2$ inch) cubes and fry off in a little olive oil till lightly coloured. Transfer into a moderate oven for 10-12 minutes until the flesh is tender. Meanwhile gently sweat the diced onion in the butter till the onion is soft but not coloured.

5 Add the rice to the onions, raise the heat and toast till the rice is shiny and translucent. Lower the heat and begin to add the stock, a ladleful at a time. Stir into the rice and wait for it to become completely absorbed before you add the next one.

6 Once the rice is cooked (al dente) and of the correct texture, fold in the mozzarella, parmesan and butternut squash and cook for 2 minutes more. Serve immediately on a hot plate, drizzle the pesto around the risotto and top off with a small pile of crisp shallots.

Risotto Mantecato

INGREDIENTS

serves 4

350g (12oz) risotto rice

1 shallot

2 tbsp olive oil

1 litre (1³/₄ pints) chicken
   stock

100g (4oz) good meat
   stock (optional)

50g (2oz) parmesan
   cheese, grated

100g (4oz) salted butter

150g (5oz) smoked buffalo
   mozzarella

salt & pepper

METHOD

1 Chop the shallot very finely and fry in the olive oil. Add the rice and cook for 2-3 minutes, mixing all the time.

2 Boil the chicken stock, add half to the rice and cook for 15 minutes, adding the remainder of the stock a little at a time.

3 Remove from the heat and leave to cool for 2-3 minutes. Then start mixing vigourously with a wooden spoon while adding first the mozzarella, then the parmesan, and then the butter.

4 Season with salt and pepper and serve.

Note: If you want to use the meat stock as well, add half to the rice after the parmesan, and pour the rest on top when serving.

Spiced Tomato & Mozzarella Risotto

(recipe on following page)

Spiced Tomato & Mozzarella Risotto

INGREDIENTS

serves 6

8 plum tomatoes

1 litre (1³/₄ pints) fresh
chicken stock

100g (4oz) butter

1 sweet white onion, finely
chopped

1 tsp harissa

zest of half a lemon

1 clove garlic, finely
chopped

400g (16oz) Carnaroli rice

300g (12oz) buffalo
mozzarella

6 tbsp grated parmesan

METHOD

1 *Preheat the grill. Grill the whole tomatoes for 5 minutes on each side or until the skin is blistered and the flesh is soft. Transfer to a liquidizer and blitz to a purée. Push the purée through a sieve to remove the skin and seeds. Season and set aside.*

2 *In a medium saucepan bring the stock to a boil and keep at a gentle simmer. In a wide stainless steel pan melt the butter and add the onion, harissa, lemon zest and garlic. Cook over a gentle heat for 5 minutes. Add the rice and continue to cook for a further 2 minutes. Now add the fresh tomato purée and stir continuously until the rice has absorbed the purée.*

3 *Once the purée has been absorbed, add the hot stock a ladleful at a time, allowing the rice to absorb each dose of stock before the next one is added (this process should take about 15-18 minutes).*

4 *Remove from the heat, stir in half of the parmesan and check the seasoning. Finally cut the mozzarella into small cubes, return the pan to the heat and fold in the mozzarella. As soon as the mozzarella is heated through and has started to go stringy it is ready to serve. Divide onto 6 plates and sprinkle over the remaining parmesan.*

Saffron & Mozzarella Risotto with Rocket

METHOD

1 Gently fry the shallots in 120g (4¹/₂ oz) butter for 4-5 minutes until they start to colour, then add the rice and fry for a further 3 or 4 minutes, stirring so that all the rice is coated with butter.

2 Then add the saffron-infused chicken stock to about 400ml (16 floz) of the normal chicken stock. Bring this to the boil. Once the stock is boiling the rest of the cooking process will take about 15 minutes.

3 Start adding the rest of the chicken stock to the rice bit by bit, stirring the whole time and only adding more stock when the rice has absorbed the previous ladleful. Continue with this until the rice is cooked and the stock gone.

4 Season with salt and pepper and stir in a 50g (2oz) knob of butter. You are now ready to serve, but just before you do, stir in the mozzarella. This only needs to go in 1 minute before you serve, so it is just melting.

5 In another pan wilt the rocket in a bit of olive oil. Then serve the risotto in a bowl with a spoonful of wilted rocket on top and sprinkle with parmesan.

INGREDIENTS

serves 6

750ml (1¹/₄ pints) chicken stock

300g (12oz) rice

170g (6oz) butter

100g (4oz) shallots

1 tsp saffron threads infused in 25ml (1floz) of the chicken stock

3 x 100g (4oz) balls buffalo mozzarella cut into 1cm (¹/₂ inch) cubes

6 handfuls rocket salad

3 tbsp grated parmesan

Saffron & Mozzarella Risotto with

Rocket (recipe on preceding page)

Red Onions & Buffalo Mozzarella on a Bed of Wild Rice

INGREDIENTS

serves 4

150g (5oz) wild rice

(cooked in salted water

for 15 minutes)

400g (16oz) mozzarella

150g (5oz) red onions

100g (4oz) broad beans

BASIL DRESSING

100ml (4floz) olive oil

20ml (½floz) lemon

juice

salt & pepper

50g (2oz) basil

METHOD

1 *To make the dressing, blend all the ingredients together and use some of it to dress the cooked rice.*

2 *Cut the onions thinly into rings and dress.*

3 *Cut the mozzarella into 4 thick slices and dress.*

4 *Cook the broad beans in salted water, allow to cool, then dress.*

5 *On each plate, arrange a patty of cold rice. Place the mozzarella and onions on top. Arrange the broad beans and the rest of the dressing around this.*

Mozzarella, Basil & Tomato Risotto

METHOD

1 *In advance, thinly slice one of the plum tomatoes (unskinned), sprinkle with a little salt and leave on a wire tray overnight to dry.*

2 *Plunge the remaining plum tomatoes in a small pan of boiling water for 10 seconds. Remove the tomatoes and put them into iced water. When they are cold, peel and quarter, remove seeds and cut into 3cm (1¼ inch) chunks.*

3 *Melt half the butter in a thick-bottomed pan. Add the shallots, garlic and rice and sweat for 3-4 minutes.*

4 *Add half the vegetable stock to the pan, stirring constantly to stop the rice from sticking. Gradually add the remaining stock. The rice is ready when almost all the stock has been absorbed and the grains are al dente.*

5 *Remove from the heat, add the double cream, chopped mozzarella, diced plum tomatoes, remaining butter, and most of the picked basil, leaving a little for garnishing.*

6 *On serving, garnish with the remaining basil and the sliced, dried tomato.*

INGREDIENTS

serves 6

300g (12oz) Arborio or risotto rice

50g (2oz) unsalted butter

2 shallots, peeled and chopped

1 clove garlic, peeled and chopped

1 litre (1¾ pints) vegetable stock

200ml (8floz) double cream

100g (4oz) buffalo mozzarella, diced

1 small bunch fresh basil leaves, picked

5 plum tomatoes

Risotto with Pancetta Affumicata, Buffalo Mozzarella & Savoy Cabbage

INGREDIENTS

serves 4

400g (16oz) Arborio rice

1¹/₂ litres (2¹/₃ pints) fresh
  chicken stock, kept
  simmering

1 medium onion

¹/₂ head Savoy cabbage,
  shredded into tiny pieces

100g (4oz) unsalted butter

150g (5oz) reggiano
  parmesan

2 x 125g (4¹/₂oz) balls
  buffalo mozzarella, cut
  into small pieces

100g (4oz) pancetta
  affumicata

1 glass dry white wine

1 clove garlic, sliced

METHOD

1 Slice pancetta into matchsticks, and fry with sliced garlic until golden. Toss in the shredded Savoy cabbage, place a lid on the pan and steam for about 5 minutes. Season, remove from heat and set aside.

2 Chop red onion very finely. Heat heavy-based saucepan and melt butter.

When the butter starts to foam, add the chopped onion and cook on reduced heat for 2-3 minutes until soft but not brown.

3 Add the rice, and stir continuously for about 3 minutes until the rice becomes translucent. Then pour in the white wine and allow to absorb. Start adding the simmering stock to the rice, ladle by ladle, stirring continuously. The rice is cooked when it has a thick creamy consistency, and an even, al dente bite to the grain.

4 Incorporate the cooked pancetta and Savoy cabbage mixture. Fold in the parmesan, season, and serve.

Pesce e Crostacei

Stefan Cavallini / THE HALKIN

Caponatina of Aubergine, Prawns & Mozzarella

Simone Cerea / CARAVAGGIO

Buffalo Mozzarella with a Fan of Smoked Salmon & White Chicory

Henry Harris / FIFTH FLOOR, HARVEY NICHOLS

Treccine Dressed with Anchovies, Onion & Lemon

Alberico Penati / HARRY'S BAR

Bocconcini & Caviar

Alberico Penati / ANNABEL'S

Mozzarella & Crab Layers with a Saffron Sauce

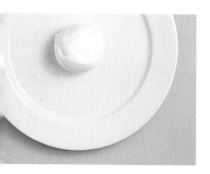

Caponatina of Aubergine, Prawns & Mozzarella

INGREDIENTS

serves 4

2 large aubergines

20 large prawns

2 x 150g (5oz) balls
    buffalo mozzarella

50g (2oz) celery, diced
    and blanched

50g (2oz) olives, seeded
    and chopped

20g (¹/₂ oz) capers

20g (¹/₂ oz) chopped onion

20g (¹/₂ oz) pine kernels

2 tomatoes, chopped

juice of half a lemon

10ml (¹/₄ floz) squid ink

3 tbsp olive oil

METHOD

1 Cut the aubergines into large cubes, approximately 1cm (¹/₂ inch) in size and cook them in a nonstick pan with a pinch of salt.

2 Sauté the onion in a tbsp of olive oil, then add the celery, aubergine, olives, capers, pine kernels and tomato. When these ingredients have softened add the mozzarella, cut into cubes, at the last minute. Remove from heat and reserve.

3 Heat some more olive oil and cook the prawns. Meanwhile mix the remainder of the oil with the squid ink and lemon juice.

4 To serve, arrange the aubergine and mozzarella mixture in the centre of each plate. Then arrange 5 prawns per plate around the edge and drizzle with the squid ink dressing.

Buffalo Mozzarella with a Fan of Smoked Salmon & White Chicory

METHOD

1 *Pan fry the white chicory leaves until crispy and golden. Lay the leaves on the plate alternately with the smoked salmon in a fan shape.*

2 *Cut the mozzarella into large slices, sprinkle with finely chopped basil, salt and pepper. Place mozzarella slices at the base of each chicory and salmon fan.*

3 *Skin the red pepper carefully with a potato peeler and remove the seeds. Slice into 6 pieces. Place the finely chopped shallot in a pan with a spoonful of olive oil and a knob of butter.*

Add the pepper and gently fry for 10-15 minutes until softened.

4 *Place the contents of the frying pan into a blender with the remaining ingredients. Blend until smooth and creamy. Add salt and pepper to taste and use to decorate the plate.*

INGREDIENTS

serves 4

250g (10oz) buffalo mozzarella

160g (5oz) smoked salmon

leaves of 2 white chicory

salt & pepper

SAUCE

1 large red pepper

5g ($^1/_8$oz) fresh tarragon

$^1/_2$ bunch fresh basil

$^1/_2$ shallot, finely chopped

2 tbsp vegetable stock

2 tbsp olive oil

knob of butter

INGREDIENTS

serves 4-6

1 medium red onion

1 large lemon

12 best quality salted
   anchovy fillets

4 slices sourdough bread

1 tbsp olive oil

2 garlic cloves, peeled

4 buffalo mozzarella
   treccine

1 tsp fresh thyme

2 tbsp coarsely chopped
   flat-leaf parsley

1 tbsp extra virgin olive oil

freshly ground black pepper

Treccine Dressed with Anchovies, Onion & Lemon

METHOD

1 Peel the red onion and slice as thinly as possible, then place in a bowl of iced water for at least 30 minutes.

2 Remove the pith and rind from the lemon, segment it and then coarsely chop the flesh. Split the anchovy fillets lengthwise into thin strands and keep both to one side.

3 Preheat a ridged cast-iron grill, brush the slices of bread with some olive oil and grill until nicely browned. While the bread is still hot rub each slice on one side with the garlic cloves in order to flavour the bread. Then cut the bread into strips.

4 To serve, place 1 treccine on each plate, scatter over the anchovy, chopped lemon and thyme. Remove the onion from the iced water, shake it dry and arrange a tangle of it on each cheese. Scatter the grilled bread and chopped parsley around the edge and finish it off with a good drizzle of the extra virgin oil and generous milling of black pepper.

Bocconcini & Caviar

METHOD

1 *Place the boiled spinach and cress in a blender and mix on high speed to make the purée. Add a tbsp of olive oil, salt and pepper and stir to a smooth consistency.*

2 *Place equal portions of caviar on each plate, shaping into a circular patty. Shape the purée into mounds and place 3 around the caviar.*

3 *Garnish each mound with the tomato, chives and olive oil. Place a bocconcini on top of each caviar patty and drizzle with olive oil.*

INGREDIENTS

Serves 4

150g (5oz) Osietra caviar

4 mozzarella bocconcini

150g (5oz) purée made
   with half watercress and
   half boiled spinach

chives for garnishing

1 tomato, cut into 25mm
   (2 inch) fingers

50ml (2floz) olive oil.

Mozzarella & Crab Layers with a Saffron Sauce

INGREDIENTS

serves 4

6 x 150g (5oz) balls
    buffalo mozzarella

240g (10oz) crab meat

70g (3oz) mirepoix of
    vegetables (green beans,
    carrots and asparagus)

flat-leaf parsley to garnish

CITRONETTE

100ml (4floz) olive oil

20ml (½floz) lemon juice

salt & pepper

SAFFRON SAUCE

200g (8oz) mayonnaise

2 saffron strands

70g (3floz) cream

METHOD

1 *Cut the mozzarella into even slices.*

2 *Mix the citronette ingredients, and dress the crab.*

3 *Dice the vegetables for the mirepoix and blanch, adding saffron for a few seconds at the end. Sauté the vegetables lightly and mix with the crab.*

4 *Boil the cream and add the saffron for a moment. Remove saffron, add the cream to the mayonnaise and mix well.*

5 *On each plate, arrange a slice of mozzarella, and on top of that a layer of crab. Keep alternating until you have 3 layers of mozzarella and 3 layers of crab. Spoon the sauce around it, and garnish with parsley.*

Carne

Henry Harris / FIFTH FLOOR, HARVEY NICHOLS
Burrata ai Tartufi Bianchi with Prosciutto & Deepfried Artichokes

Paul Wilson / GEORGES
Warm Asparagus, Prosciutto & Mozzarella

Antonello Tagliabue / BICE
Veal Cutlet Stuffed with Mozzarella & Porcini

Simone Cerea / CARAVAGGIO
Veal Escalope with Fresh Spinach & Mozarella

Quinto Cecchetti / LA FAMIGLIA
Veal Escalope with Aubergine & Melting Mozzarella

John Torode / MEZZO
Baked Mozzarella Wrapped in Prosciutto

Dean Carr / THE AVENUE
Bruschetta of Parma Ham & Mozzarella with Onion Marmalade

Sally Clarke / CLARKE'S
San Daniele Prosciutto with Buffalo Mozzarella, Figs & Balsamic Dressing

Burrata ai Tartufi Bianchi with Prosciutto & Deepfried Artichokes

INGREDIENTS

serves 4

2 Burrata ai Tartufi Bianchi

4 slices Carpegna
   prosciutto

8 cooked baby artichokes,
   bought from delicatessen

1 tsp mascarpone cheese

200ml (8floz) Barbera
   d'Alba red wine

100ml (4floz) extra virgin
   olive oil

250ml (10floz) milk

250g (10oz) seasoned flour

oil for deepfrying

1 small packet of chives

3 tbsp chopped shallots

METHOD

1 *Place the red wine and shallots in a small saucepan, bring it to the boil and reduce by half. Remove from the heat and whisk in the mascarpone followed by a steady stream of olive oil. Season and set aside.*

2 *Halve the artichokes, pass them through the milk and seasoned flour twice, and then deepfry until golden. Drain and place on some kitchen paper and season with a little salt.*

3 *Place the Burrata in the centre of a serving platter. Arrange the prosciutto and artichokes around the cheese. Finally drizzle over the dressing, sprinkle with the chives, and place the plate in the middle of the table with a serving spoon.*

Note: Burrata ai Tartufi Bianchi is a mozzarella parcel stuffed with creamy, shredded mozzarella and sometimes flavoured with white truffle oil. It can be ordered from a specialist Italian grocer. If the Burrata is unavailable, substitute with buffalo mozzarella, drizzled with a little white truffle oil if desired.

Warm Asparagus, Prosciutto & Mozzarella

METHOD

1 Peel asparagus spears 2 inches from the top, rinse, and cook in boiling salted water for roughly 4 minutes until tender, then refresh quickly in iced water. Keep warm until ready to serve.

2 Now take the mozzarella and slice each ball into 3 portions, season lightly with salt and pepper, and place a sage leaf on top of each slice of mozzarella.

3 Take each slice of prosciutto and slice lengthways 3 times into thin strips. Place 1 slice of mozzarella at one end of each strip of prosciutto, and roll so that the prosciutto is wrapped around the centre of the mozzarella.

4 In a hot pan quickly fry the asparagus spears in a little oil and butter until well-coloured. Season and keep warm.

5 Now place a baking tray under a hot grill with a generous amount of cooking oil.

6 When very hot, carefully place mozzarella slices on the tray, turning over after 30 seconds. Remove from direct heat once all of the mozzarella has been sealed.

7 Now gently heat up a small frying pan over a moderate heat. Meanwhile arrange the cooked warm asparagus on a plate, arrange the mozzarella slices on top and keep plates warm in a low oven.

8 In your warm frying pan add the unsalted butter and melt until it starts to bubble. Add the sage leaves and continue to heat until they begin to brown. Add lemon juice, salt and pepper, then remove from the direct heat.

9 Remove plates of asparagus and mozzarella from the oven and generously spoon the sage butter all over and around the asparagus, then drizzle over a little of the balsamic vinegar.

INGREDIENTS

serves 4

4 x 100g (4oz) balls buffalo mozzarella

8 thin slices prosciutto

20 asparagus spears

50g (2oz) sage leaves

170g (6oz) butter

3 tbsp lemon juice

aged balsamic vinegar

Veal Cutlet Stuffed with Mozzarella & Porcini

INGREDIENTS

serves 4

4 veal cutlets
  (on the bone)

2 x 100g (4oz) balls
  buffalo mozzarella

150g (5oz) of fresh porcini
  mushrooms

24 basil leaves

4 tbsp grated parmesan

2 tomatoes, peeled
  and diced

1 garlic clove

2 tbsp chopped parsley

200g (8oz) mixed salad
  leaves (endive, radicchio,
  lettuce, rocket)

1 bunch of rosemary

150g (5oz) butter

200ml (8floz) olive oil

METHOD

1 *Slice the veal cutlets in half lengthways and flatten each half slightly. Season with salt and pepper.*

2 *Slice the mushrooms. Sauté the porcini in olive oil with the garlic and parsley.*

3 *Dice the mozzarella and place onto one half of each cutlet, along with a few pieces of tomato, some parmesan and half of the mushrooms. Place the other half of the veal cutlet on top, sealing the edges by pressing down with the back of a knife blade.*

4 *Braise the cutlets in a frying pan with oil, butter and the rosemary. Finish the cooking in a preheated oven at 190°C (375°F) for 8-9 minutes.*

5 *Place the remaining mushrooms into the frying pan with the veal juices still in it. Add a spoonful of butter and simmer.*

6 *Sauté the salad leaves in a frying pan with a spoonful of olive oil and arrange a bed of them on 4 serving plates. Place the veal in the middle and spoon over the porcini mushroom sauce.*

INGREDIENTS

serves 4

4 x 150g (5oz) slices of
   top rump veal

160g (5oz) fresh boiled
   spinach

20g (1/2 oz) parmesan
   cheese

160g (5oz) mozzarella

2 tomatoes, skinned

dash of dry white wine

GARNISH

4 medium tomatoes

40g (1oz) soft bread
   crumbs

1 tbsp olive oil

5g (1/8 oz) finely chopped
   parsley

2 anchovy fillets, chopped

1/2 clove garlic, chopped

Veal Escalope with Fresh Spinach & Mozzarella

METHOD

1 *Beat out the slices of veal and shallow fry in very hot oil. Remove the remainder of the oil and add a dash of dry white wine, frying for a further 2 minutes. Take out the veal, reserving the stock for later.*

2 *Place the slices of veal on a baking tray and top with spinach, a pinch of salt, parmesan cheese, 2 slices of mozzarella and 2 quarters of skinned tomato.*

3 *Slice the tops off the 4 tomatoes and deseed. Mix the breadcrumbs together with the olive oil, chopped parsley, anchovies and garlic, and place inside the tomatoes. Place on tray with veal and cook in oven pre-heated to 200°C (400°F) for 6-8 minutes until the cheese is golden brown.*

4 *Serve 1 slice of veal and 1 tomato on each plate, surrounded with a little of the remaining stock.*

Veal Escalope with Aubergine & Melting Mozzarella

INGREDIENTS

serves 4

4 veal escalopes

1 medium aubergine

2 x 150g (5oz) balls
buffalo mozzarella, sliced

250g (9oz) flour

dash of white wine

5 tbsp olive oil

fresh tomato sauce (see
recipe on page 155)

METHOD

1 Coat veal escalopes with a light dusting of flour. Then fry on both sides in a little oil, adding a dash of white wine. Set aside.

2 Slice aubergine lengthways and fry in olive oil until golden on both sides. Remove from pan.

3 Place a slice of aubergine on each piece of veal. Then spread mozzarella slices on top. Put under the grill for a few minutes until the cheese has melted. Remove from grill, spoon over the tomato sauce and serve.

Baked Mozzarella Wrapped in Prosciutto

METHOD

1 Heat 1 tbsp of the olive oil in a pan and sweat the shallot and garlic over a low heat until soft.

2 Add the vinegar and cook for a further 3-4 minutes until reduced, then add the passata and tomatoes, and simmer for 3 minutes.

3 Add the herbs and remaining olive oil, and cook over a very low heat for 10-15 minutes, stirring occasionally, until thick and a deep red. Season to taste. Remove from the heat, allow to cool, then push through a coarse sieve and set aside.

4 Preheat the oven to 150°C (300°F). Season the mozzarella with black pepper and roll up in the prosciutto, allowing 2 slices per ball of cheese.

5 Heat the oil in a large frying pan over a high heat until just smoking. Place the parcels in the pan and sear, turning constantly, until the outsides are well-coloured, for about 1 minute. Transfer the parcels to a baking dish and cook in the oven for 5-6 minutes.

6 Spoon tomato sauce in the centre of individual plates and sprinkle with the chopped basil and tarragon. Set a mozzarella parcel on top, drizzle with olive oil and serve.

INGREDIENTS

serves 4

4 x 125g (5oz) balls buffalo mozzarella

8 thin slices prosciutto

1¹/₂ tbsp vegetable oil

TOMATO SAUCE

4 tbsp extra virgin olive oil

1 shallot, finely chopped

1 garlic clove, chopped

1 tbsp champagne vinegar

half cup passata (tomato puree)

6 plum tomatoes, peeled and deseeded

5 basil leaves

5 tarragon leaves

sea salt

freshly ground black pepper

TO SERVE

a little chopped basil and tarragon

olive oil to drizzle

Bruschetta of Parma Ham & Mozzarella with Onion Marmalade

INGREDIENTS

serves 4

3 white onions, peeled

1 clove garlic, chopped

1 pinch thyme, picked

1 bay leaf

10g (¹/₂ oz) mustard seeds

50ml (2floz) red wine

50ml (2floz) red wine
   vinegar

50g (2oz) brown sugar

50g (2oz) butter

150g (5oz) buffalo
   mozzarella

200g (8oz) Parma ham,
   sliced

2 bunches fresh rocket

1 medium focaccia or any
   good 'farmhouse' bread

ground black pepper

METHOD

1 Cut the onions in half using a sharp knife. Remove the roots and slice thinly.

2 Melt the butter in a thick-bottomed pan, adding the sliced onions, chopped garlic, picked thyme, bay leaf and mustard seeds. Stir continuously for 15-20 minutes, allowing the onions to turn a golden brown.

3 Add the sugar, red wine and red wine vinegar and cover with greaseproof paper. Reduce the heat and cook for 30-40 minutes to allow the marmalade to thicken.

4 Cut the mozzarella into 4 thick slices. Cut the focaccia into squares and toast.

5 To assemble, spoon the onion marmalade onto a plate and place a piece of focaccia on top with a few rocket leaves. Arrange the sliced Parma ham and mozzarella on top. To finish, add a twist of black pepper.

San Daniele Prosciutto with Mozzarella, Figs & Balsamic Dressing

INGREDIENTS

serves 6

2 tbsp pine nuts

6 ripe green or black figs

6 x 150g (5oz) balls
  buffalo mozzarella,
  drained of excess milk

12 generous slices of
  San Daniele prosciutto

6 bread sticks

DRESSING

60ml (2oz) extra virgin
  olive oil

3 tsp balsamic vinegar

rock salt

freshly ground black
  pepper

METHOD

1 Mix balsamic dressing ingredients together and season to taste.

2 Place pine nuts on a baking sheet and bake in a medium oven until golden. Allow to cool.

3 Wipe figs and trim tops away. Cut into quarters.

4 Cut mozzarella as desired and arrange neatly with the slices of San Daniele prosciutto and figs.

5 Sprinkle with pine nuts and drizzle with dressing. Serve with a breadstick.

glossary

Aioli

Garlic mayonnaise ideally suited to use in fish soups, fish, egg and vegetable dishes.

Anchoiade

A paste of anchovies, garlic and olive oil, used as a spread or condiment.

Ballotine

A roll traditionally made from a poultry or game bird cut that has been boned and stuffed. It may be served hot with a sauce or served cold in aspic.

Beignet

A French-style fritter, usually of deep-fried choux pastry.

Brioche

Bread of a rich yeasty dough, using a higher proportion of eggs and butter than usual.

Ingredients (makes 1 loaf)
4 tbsp milk, warmed
1 1/2 tbsp fresh yeast or
1 tbsp dried yeast
1 tbsp flour
2 tbsp caster sugar
625g (1 lb 1/4 oz) unbleached plain flour plus extra for dusting
1 tbsp salt
4 medium eggs, beaten
1 egg yolk beaten with 1 tbsp milk for glazing
275g (11oz) unsalted butter, softened

Method
1. Place the warmed milk in a small bowl and whisk in the yeast. Allow to stand for 5 minutes. Stir in the flour and sugar and set aside for 30 minutes.
2. Place the flour, salt and sugar in a mixing bowl and make a well in the centre. Pour in the yeasted milk and the eggs. Using your fingers, lightly bring the flour and liquid together, until a dough begins to form, then turn out on to a floured board and knead for 15-20 minutes, until elastic and smooth.
3. Gently beat the softened butter with the back of a spoon until smooth, then add gradually to the dough, about 2 tbsp at a time. Knead the dough between your fingertips to incorporate the butter until thoroughly combined. Repeat until all the butter has been added. Cover bowl with a clean cloth and leave in a warm place for 2 hours or until the dough has doubled in size. Knock back by either punching down or turning over on itself. Cover and rest in the refrigerator for several hours, preferably overnight.

Buffalo Mozzarella

A soft cheese made from buffalo milk, a specialty of Naples

Caponata

Italian-style ratatouille from Sicily, traditionally based around a mixture of onions, celery, tomatoes and aubergines.

Carta Musica

A traditional Sardinian bread, also known as Pane Carasau, made without yeast and characterised by its crisp, paper-thin texture and golden colour.

It is cooked in large rounds on the baker's slab and keeps well over long periods. Carta Musica refers to the thin parchment used classically for writing music.

Ciabatta

A long oval bread resembling the shape of a 'ciabatta', a kind of homely slipper. The dough contains more water than required for most breads, and takes especially long to rise, creating a light bread with thin crust.

Coulibiac

A classic Russian dish in which layers of fish, vegetables and eggs are wrapped in brioche pastry.

Focaccia

A thick, flat Italian bread made with flour, salt, yeast and water. It is often flavoured with different ingredients such as olive oil, herbs, eggs or cheese.

Girolle

Mushroom variety native to France, featuring a small head and long stem.

Mayonnaise

A cold dressing made from egg yolks. Mayonnaise ingredients should be kept at room temperature prior to mixing:

Ingredients

2 egg yolks
300ml ($^1/_2$ pint) extra virgin olive oil
1 tbsp lemon juice
salt & pepper

Method

Prepare the mayonnaise in a mixer: Place the 2 egg yolks (these must be at room temperature) in the mixing bowl, add a pinch of salt, pepper, and half the lemon juice and start mixing at medium speed. Add the olive oil a little bit at a time until it has all been absorbed into a thick mixture.

Orecchiette

A pasta originating from the Apulia region of Italy. The word translates as 'little ears', referring to the small, husk-like shape of the noodles.

Pesto

An Italian sauce particularly associated with the province of Liguria, renowned for its sweet basil and extra virgin olive oil.

Ingredients

50g (2oz) fresh basil leaves
25g (1oz) pine nuts
3 cloves garlic, peeled
200ml (8floz) olive oil
2 tbsp grated Parmesan cheese

Method

Purée the basil, pine nuts, garlic, cheese and a small quantity of the oil in a blender. With the blender on a slow setting, gradually add the rest of the oil. Season with salt and pepper. If making by hand, use a mortar and pestle to grind the basil, garlic and pine nuts to a paste, gradually adding the cheese until the paste is smooth. Then gradually stir in the olive oil. Store in a jar with a thin layer of olive oil on top.

Porcini

Wild mushroom with a thick bulbous stem, a specialty of Tuscany. It is most commonly found in spring, between March and July, and in autumn from September to November. They are the best wild mushrooms for drying.

Rotolo

A roll of vegetables, cheese or meats wrapped in pasta or dough.

Salsify

A Mediterranean herb with an oyster-like taste, the root of the salsify plant.

Timballo

Classic Italian dish usually made with a mixture of meat and vegetables cooked in a mould lined with pasta.

Tomato Sauce

A basic Italian-style recipe:

Ingredients

250g (10oz) tin peeled tomatoes, or fresh, peeled tomatoes
1 onion
2 cloves garlic
salt
3 tbsp olive oil

Method

Heat the oil in a frying pan and sauté chopped onions with chopped garlic until golden. Then add peeled tomatoes, salt and pepper to taste and cook for about 20 minutes until the excess water evaporates. A tsp of tomato paste or purée may be added if desired.

Treccine

A plait of soft mozzarella cheese.

contributors

Simon Arkless
OXO TOWER

- *Butternut Squash, Mozzarella*
  & Caramelised Garlic Risotto
  with Crispy Shallots & Pesto
- *Grilled Flat Mushrooms & Melted Mozzarella*
  with Sundried Pepper & Pickled Chilli Relish
- *Baked Tomatoes with Basil Cream*
  & Melted Mozzarella on Herb Crostini

Lorenzo Berni
SAN LORENZO

- *Insalata del Principe di Napoli*
- *Le Penne dei Principi di Paternó*

David Burke
LE PONT DE LA TOUR

- *Panfried Ciabatta Sandwich*
  with Buffalo Mozzarella
- *Ballotine of Grilled Vegetables*
  with Buffalo Mozzarella
- *Buffalo Mozzarella, Tomato & Pesto Tart*

Chris Benians
DAPHNE'S

- *Spaghetti alla Sorrento*
- *Buffalo Mozzarella with*
  Rolled Aubergine & Pesto
- *Buffalo Mozzarella with Peppers Piedmontese*

Dean Carr
THE AVENUE

- *Mozzarella, Basil & Tomato Risotto*
- *Grilled Vegetable & Mozzarella Salad with Roast Garlic*
- *Brioche with Peppers, Aubergines & Mozzarella*

Stefano Cavallini
THE HALKIN

- *Ravioli alla Mozzarella*
- *Fiori di Zucchina*
- *Caponatina of Aubergine, Prawns & Mozzarella*

Quinto Cecchetti
LA FAMIGLIA

- *Veal Escalope with Grilled Aubergine & Mozzarella*

Simone Cerea
CARAVAGGIO

- *Buffalo Mozzarella with a Fan of Smoked Salmon & White Chicory*
- *Veal Escalope with Fresh Spinach & Mozzarella*
- *Fresh Linguine with Asparagus, Sundried Tomatoes & Smoked Mozzarella*

Alberto Chiappa
MONTPELIANO

- *Insalata alla Sophia*
- *Risotto Mantecato*
- *Mozzarella, Asparagus, Raisins & Pine Nuts with Vinaigrette al Peperone*

Sally Clarke
CLARKE'S

- *Baked Shallot & Oven Dried Tomato Focaccia with Bocconcini*
- *Grilled Finger Aubergine with Purple Basil & Mozzarella*
- *San Daniele Prosciutto with Mozzarella, Figs & Balsamic Dressing*

Henry Harris
FIFTH FLOOR
HARVEY NICHOLS

- *Spiced Tomato & Mozzarella Risotto*
- *Treccine Dressed with Anchovies, Onion & Lemon*
- *Burrata ai Tartufi Bianchi with Prosciutto & Deepfried Artichokes*

Henrik Iversen
QUAGLINO'S

- *Warm Salad of Buffalo Mozzarella & Girolles with Cabernet Vinegar*
- *Buffalo Mozzarella with Couscous, Lemon, Parsley & Capers*
- *Aubergine & Buffalo Mozzarella Beignet with Salsify & Balsamic*

Michael Moore
BLUEBIRD

- *Flatbread with Bocconcini, Spices & Anchovies*
- *Rotolo of Woodroasted Aubergine with Peppers & Brioche*
- *Polenta, Mozzarella & Parma Ham Sandwich*

Matthew Harris
BIBENDUM

- *Spiced Artichoke Salad*
- *Fried Mozzarella with Anchovy Dressing, French Bean Salad & Parmesan*
- *Saffron & Mozzarella Risotto with Rocket*

Alastair Little
ALASTAIR LITTLE

- *Grilled Flatbread with Buffalo Mozzarella & Rosemary*
- *Gâteau of Grilled Vegetables & Mozzarella*

Alberico Penati
HARRY'S BAR & ANNABEL'S

- *Chilled Tomato & Mozzarella Salad*
- *Smoked Buffalo Mozzarella with Porcini Mushrooms*
- *Sculpted Vegetables with Bocconcini*
- *Red Onions & Buffalo Mozzarella on a Bed of Wild Rice*
- *Bocconcini & Caviar*
- *Mozzarella & Crab Layers with a Saffron Sauce*

Theo Randall
RIVER CAFE

◆ *Rigatoni with Plum Tomato Sauce, Marjoram, Buffalo Mozzarella & Pecorino*

◆ *Baked Buffalo Mozzarella on Pasta Frolla*

◆ *Risotto with Pancetta Affumicata, Buffalo Mozzarella & Savoy Cabbage*

Antonello Tagliabue
BICE

◆ *Foccacia Toscana with Mozzarella, Roast Peppers & Basil Cream*

◆ *Timballo of Aubergines & Orecchiette Pasta with a Mozzarella & Tomato Sauce*

◆ *Veal Cutlet Stuffed with Mozzarella & Porcini*

Paul Wilson
GEORGES (MELBOURNE)

◆ *Crescenta with Mozzarella, Roasted Peppers & Anchoiade*

◆ *Seared Tomatoes, Caponata & Mozzarella*

Nino Sassu
ASSAGGI

◆ *Aubergine Salad with Carta Musica*

John Torode
MEZZO

◆ *Roast Tomato Salad with Buffalo Mozzarella*

◆ *Brioche with Peppers, Aubergine & Mozzarella*

◆ *Baked Mozzarella Wrapped in Prosciutto*

index

anchovies
anchoiade 42-3
dressing 43, 86-7
with flatbread 34-5
with treccine 130-1
artichokes
deepfried 138-9
in ravioli 62-3
in salad 22-3, 18-20
asparagus
with linguine 56-7
*with mozzarella, raisins
  & pine nuts 74-5*
*with prosciutto &
  mozzarella 140-1*
in salad 28-9
aubergines
in beignet 96-7
with brioche 40-1
as caponata 76-7, 126-7
grilled, with mozzarella 90-2
with mozzarella and pesto 78-9
with Orecchiette pasta 60-1
in salad 30-1
with veal 146-7
in vegetable gâteau 84-5
woodroasted 48-9
avocados *in salad 21, 24-5*

basil
with aubergine 90-2
with baked tomatoes 94-5
with focaccia 38-9
in risotto 120-1
beans
in pâté 100-1
in salad 86-7
bocconcini
with caviar 132-3
with vegetables 98-9
brioches *40-1, 48-9*

cabbage *in risotto 122-3*
caviar *132-3*

courgettes and flowers *88-9*
couscous *82-3*
crab *134-5*

fennel *in salad 28-9*
figs *with prosciutto 152-3*
focaccia *38-9, 45-7, 50-1*

garlic
in grilled vegetable gâteau 84-5
in risotto 108-9
roasted 16-17

linguine *56-7*

mozzarella
history 4-7
making 8-11
name 4
mushrooms
grilled 102-3
Porcini with mozzarella 93
Porcini with veal 142-3
in warm salad 26-7

onions
in caponata 76-7
in marmalade 150-1
with treccine 130-1
with wild rice 118-19

pancetta affumicata
in risotto 122-3
penne *68-9*
peppers
with brioche 40-1, 48-9
in crescenta 42-3
with focaccia 38-9
Piedmontese 80-1
in relish 102-3
in salad 24-5
in vegetable gâteau 84-5
in vinaigrette 74-5
pesto *79*
in mozzarella & tomato tart 104-5
in risotto 108-9
pine nuts
with mozzarella & asparagus 74-5

polenta
*as sandwich with mozzarella
  & Parma ham 52-3*
prawns
*in caponatina with aubergine
  & mozzarella 126-7*

ravioli *62-3*
rigatoni
*with plum tomato sauce,
  mozzarella & Pecorino 64-5*

salmon
*smoked, with mozzarella
  & chicory 128-9*
shallots
baked in focaccia 45-7
*in risotto with butternut squash
  & mozzarella 108-9*
smoked mozzarella
with Porcini mushrooms 93
spaghetti *58-9*
spinach
with veal escalope 144-5

timballo
*of aubergines & Orecchiette
  pasta 60-1*
tomatoes
baked with mozzarella 94-5
oven dried in focaccia 45-7
*in risotto with mozzarella
  112-14; 120-1*
roasted, in salad 22-3
in salad 28-9
in sauce with rigatoni 64-5
seared, with mozzarella 76-7
with spaghetti 58-9
tomatoes, sundried
*with linguine & smoked
  mozzarella 56-7*
tuna *in salad 24-5*

veal
*with aubergine & melted
  mozzarella 146-7*
with spinach & mozzarella 144-5
*stuffed with mozzarella
  & Porcini 142-3*

acknowledgments

Francesco Moncada di Paternò thanks: Caseificio Flli. Fierro, in particular Giuseppe Fierro and Marco Fossataro; Dott. Nicola Damiani; Dott. Enzo Spagnoli; and Alan Parker from Central Scientific Laboratories. Kind thanks also to: Simon Hopkinson; La Picena, London; Kevin Gould; and Jario Chamorro-Rojas.

Sian Irvine would like to thank: Jake Curtis; Rebecca Wingrave; Steve Shipman; and Anna and Derek Irvine.

Buffalo Mozzarella supplied by Franceschiello/Blue U.K. Ltd. 8 Talina Centre, 23A Bagleys Lane, London SW6 2BW. T. 0171 610 6155. F. 0171 610 6133.

Additional photographs supplied by: The Hutchison Library
© Robert Aberman: p. 4, 6
Alessandro Melodia: p. 7, 9tr, 9bl, 10tl, 11